50 FOOTY YARNS

HALF A CHICKEN & CHIPS

Published by:
Wilkinson Publishing Pty Ltd
ACN 006 042 173
PO Box 24135 Melbourne Victoria, Australia 3001
Ph: +61 3 9654 5446
www.wilkinsonpublishing.com.au
enquiries@wilkinsonpublishing.com.au

Also by the Coodabeen Champions: *Coodabeen Champions: 40 Footy Seasons*

www.coodabeens.com.au

coodabeens
thecoodabeenchampions
Coodabeens

A catalogue record for this book is available from the National Library of Australia

Planned date of publication: 08-2021
Title: Half A Chicken & Chips — 50 Footy Yarns
ISBN(s): 9781925927696: Printed — Paperback

Front cover photograph Michael Willson, AFL Photos.
Back cover photograph Damian Rabbitt.
Cartoons by Paul Harvey.

Design: Michael Bannenberg
Printed in Australia by Griffin Press, a part of Ovato

CONTENTS

NICKNAME GLOSSARY

Banksy	Denis Banks
Barass	Ron Barassi
Big Carl	Carl Ditterich
Boomer	Brent Harvey
Boothy	Doug Booth
Buster	Graham Harland
Christmas	Wayne Carroll
Cornesy	Graham Cornes
Cowboy	Kevin Neale
Crackers	Peter Keenan
Crazy Horse	Gary Cowton
Cuddles	Ray Ball
Daics	Peter Daicos
Doc	Tony Clarkson
Doc	Darren Wheildon
Gags	Adrian Gallagher
GR	Graeme Richmond
Gunner	John Scarlett
Hassa	Harold Mann
Huddo	Peter Hudson
Jack	John Cahill
Jacko	Mark Jackson
Jezza	Alex Jesaulenko
Kanga	John Kennedy
Knightsy	Peter Knights
Kochie	David Koch
Moorey	Peter Moore
Naishy	Chris Naish
Octa	Ian Wilson
Parko	David Parkin
Percy	Peter Jones
Polly	Graham Farmer
Roachy	Michael Roach
Roosy	Paul Roos
Roundy	Barry Round
Sam	John Newman
Sellers	Mark Maclure
Sheeds	Kevin Sheedy
Sidey	Garry Sidebottom
Slug	Ray Jordon
Stewy	Ian Stewart
Superboot	Bernie Quinlan
Swamp Fox	Mike Patterson
Tilt	Rod Carter
Toddy	John Todd
Tubby	Horace Edmonds
Wallsy	Robert Walls
Wiz	Warwick Capper
Wow	Warren Jones
Yabby	Alan Jeans

FOREWORD

The interviews in this book make up just a small portion of the more than 1000 different guests we've had on our Saturday morning footy show over the past 15 or so years. But they're a good cross section of the variety of different segments we've featured over that time.

And as the producer for the majority of those years, it was my great pleasure to come up with those segment ideas and, at times, my burden to follow up by tracking guests down and convincing them to come on the show—although you'd be surprised how few showed any reluctance. I was always amazed that not one One Game Wonder I called turned me down, nor one Gardiner Medallist. Imagine in the AFL draft you were the pick before a player who went on to be a legend of the game. Now imagine a radio producer calls you out of the blue to ask you to come on and celebrate that. And yet, I can't remember anyone not hearing me out, and few, if any, who turned the opportunity down.

The reason we have such a diverse back catalogue of strange segments is largely due to my desire to outdo myself every year. How do you follow up One and Two Game Wonders? Why, with lesser-known brothers of VFL/AFL champions I suppose! And from there you roll onto the sacked coaches and their replacements, and, of course in tribute to our favourite Seven-Game-Swan, Torch, the players who kicked a goal with their first kicks. Although our campaign to re-name that 'Torching' and getting it to become part of the footy lexicon wasn't as successful as we hoped.

And then we come to the segment names. 'Oh Brother, Where Art Thou' isn't something a segment on a radio footy program would usually be called, but it was on our show in 2010, springing from the wacky mind of Billy. 'Say Hi To Your Mum For Me' came from a song on one of Champs' country albums and became a segment name in 2017.

You will find some great stories throughout this book. Some you will have heard mentioned by us multiple times, like Lady Fairfax's garden party to welcome the Swans to Sydney, or Sidey missing the bus at Lara in 1981, but there are details of those stories that even we had forgotten. And then there are the tales of injuries and almosts that seem almost impossible to have happened to one player.

And yet, over 10 minutes on a Saturday morning in a footy season, everyone had an opportunity to tell their footy story.

It has been a great privilege to track these footy stories down. We hope you enjoy them as much as we have enjoyed sharing them with you.

'Young' Andy Bellairs

You've seen the glossary of nicknames to assist with your reading of the book, now here's a rundown on the Coodabeens' nicknames to provide a little bit more help:

Richo	Jeff Richardson	*Billy*	Billy Baxter
Covey	Ian Cover	*Torch*	Torch McGee
Champs	Greg Champion	*Young Andy*	Andy Bellairs

Tommy's Been Sacked

MICK ERWIN

One of the most dramatic coach sackings in the history of footy happened in the 1982 season. Since arriving at Victoria Park in 1977, Tommy Hafey had coached the Pies to Grand Finals in four out of five seasons, including a draw in '77. However, by midseason '82 with just one win from 10 games, he was shown the door and the man who was handed the clipboard was former Richmond player, Mick Erwin. The incident also looms large in Coodabeen folklore because just weeks before Tommy gave way to Mick, Billy made the big prediction that it was all about to go down—and has lived off it ever since!

Richo: Mick Erwin, welcome to the Coodabeens.

Mick Erwin: Thank you very much.

Richo: Tell us what you remember of the chain of events that led up to you being Collingwood coach in 1982.

Mick Erwin: I guess it first started a couple of weeks before the actual decision was made. The committee had a chat to me about it and I said no way, I can't see there being anything to be gained in that, so it was a short discussion. And then two weeks later, it was on a Monday, I was working for Thorold Merrett at the time in his sports store and I was out on the road. I got back in and with no mobile phones in those days, they said the club's been trying to get you all day. This is probably at about three o'clock in the afternoon. So I rang the club and John Hickey [president] said come over straightaway and I went across to the club and went into the boardroom and they advised me that they'd dismissed Tommy and asked was I prepared to take over coaching the seniors. I had a bit of a hesitation about that but then when they mentioned that if I didn't, they were going to give it to Ronnie Richards I said well, here I am, let's have a go. I was probably on a hiding to nothing but it was not much of a choice so I decided to have a crack at it.

Billy: Did you get on the blower to Tommy Hafey at all?

Mick Erwin: No, I didn't for two to three days and then we had some feedback that Tommy wasn't happy with the way I handled it and because I played under Tom, I rang him about two weeks later and asked to have a coffee with him but he wasn't interested. He wasn't nasty or anything, he just wasn't interested and I can understand that, but at least I made the call.

Richo: You not only were a player under Tommy you also coached at Richmond. Were you coach of the Richmond reserves when Tommy was the senior coach?

Mick Erwin: No, when Barry Richardson was. When Tommy moved on to Collingwood, Barry took over as senior coach. I was a specialist coach under Tommy and Barry was reserves coach. And then Barry took over as senior coach so Tony Jewell and I coached the twos.

Richo: And I reckon Mick you were one of the most innovative coaches in the history of footy because the first time I ever saw what has come to be known as the press or the flood was a reserves game one day at the 'G, a very close game and late in the day, you had all 18 players right down one end of the ground. I'd never seen anything like it before. I reckon you invented it?

Mick: Well, I don't know about inventing it, it was probably just a tactic at the time and I didn't realise what I'd done. I think half of them got the message mixed up and half of them probably weren't supposed to be down there. But one thing I did invent when I went to the VFA at Prahran and I brought this to Collingwood when I took over, was if the ball went into the back line one side we brought it out the other. It's not quite what they do now but I called it automatically switching the play across the ground. And Daics and a few of the guys I was talking to last week at a lunch reminded me that I started that in 1982 with Collingwood well before all this other stuff. We didn't kick it backwards like they do now but it was a rule that if it came in on one half-back flank, we went across to the other side. And if you remember in those days, it would go in and it comes straight back to the pack of ruckmen. Boring.

Torch: And of course in the VFA, it was quite a weapon because you had all that space to go to because there were no wings.

Mick Erwin: It made it a real weapon, because you could just get them running down into all that space. I guess my whole aim in coaching was to get the other side to have their backs to their goals and that was one way of achieving that.

Covey: Mick, we had Gordon Towan on the program a couple of years ago.

Mick Erwin: I remember, he was a little snowy-headed wingman, I think he came from Preston.

Covey: That's right. And he said because he came down to Collingwood after the season started, one of his first nights at training was the night that you took over from Tommy and the players all gathered to run out on the training track and they all stopped in the race and let Peter Moore go on his own who was then subjected to some invective from the gathered crowd that were there. Do you remember that about that first training night under your coaching?

Mick Erwin: Absolutely, and I remember Gordon coming down

late in the year because I was coaching the twos so he would have probably played under me the week before I think. But anyway, we did all gather together. Obviously it was pretty traumatic and there was press everywhere because Tommy had been very successful and was loved by the Collingwood faithful. So it was a pretty tough gig for me. Wayne Richardson was a specialist coach, he became an assistant coach and it was good to bounce things off him. But we all ran out on the ground together, we certainly didn't let Peter run out on his own. I became pretty close to Peter over those 13 or 14 weeks as I did with a lot of the guys because we were in the trenches together and you tend to get closer. But Peter had nothing to do with Tommy being dismissed.

Champs: He was painted as a villain though, wasn't he?

Mick Erwin: He was because Tommy and he had had a pretty big argument from what I gather after the 1981 Grand Final where Pete didn't do all that well. I think he had a hamstring injury and who accepts responsibility for that? If you tell a bloke he's playing in a Grand Final, he's not going to say no is he? So they had a big argument about that at Peter's place, but in no way did Peter have any impact. And if you knew the guys on the board at the time, they wouldn't have taken any notice of Peter in relation to dismissing a coach.

Billy: Now what happened at the end of the season? You've come to the last match of the season as coach, did the board come to you and say, well enjoy your summer we'll give you a bell or did you put your hand up to continue?

Mick Erwin: Fortunately, the last game of the season we won. We won the first three games and then we struggled in between because we had something like 14 senior players injured including the Teasdales and the Peter Moores, Banksy and all of those blokes which was pretty hard. But we managed to beat Geelong down at Geelong on the last kick of the day. And after that we actually went back to the Collingwood social rooms, the big room upstairs was brand new and hadn't been open so we went back there with the president and had a reasonably good night. They came to me and said look, you're the front runner for next year, are you interested? And I said yes. And then of course they got the boot.

Torch: And then you were taken over by the Port Adelaide pusch weren't you, with Johnny Cahill and Mark Williams and the New Magpies?

Mick Erwin: That's right, but Mark was already over here. I coached Mark, he played in '82. He won a couple of Copelands, he was great but he was also out injured that year. So once the new mob came in, they weren't going to appoint me. I did get an interview which was more than Wayne Richardson and others did. Probably the amazing thing about that, and nothing against Johnny Cahill, but he came over and I don't think he'd seen a VFL game for four or five years, maybe 10 years. He didn't know the players so you thought they would have been smart enough to keep a former captain and a bloke who'd retired 12 months before and had played 17 years in the VFL around as assistant coaches, wouldn't you?

Richo: They were incredibly tumultuous times if you think over that season, to go from a Grand Final to 12 months later all the things that had happened and your involvement in it, you wouldn't see it today.

Mick Erwin: No, you wouldn't, I could write a book about what went on. While I was coaching during the year, we had the Ranald Macdonald faction coming in at training, talking to the blokes about supporting them when they went to the election and we're trying to train to play a footy game. It was disgusting.

Covey: Do you still follow the footy, Mick?

Mick Erwin: Yeah, I do. I mainly get to home games at Collingwood and I'm on the board of the former players and I still love the Tiges too. They were very, very good to me. So I still love to see them play.

Richo: Mick, it's been an absolute pleasure talking to you this morning. Thank you so much.

Mick Erwin: Okay, guys, good luck.

Champs: Good on you Mick!

GORDON TOWAN

In 2009, Gordon Towan joined us and the story he told about how he came to play two games for Collingwood in 1982 remains a favourite of the Coodabeens. Gordon's time at the Pies may have been short but it was certainly not uneventful—he spent six weeks at Collingwood in the middle of the '82 season, a period that coincided with Tommy Hafey's sensational sacking.

Richo: Gordon Towan, welcome to the Coodabeens.

Gordon Towan: G'day guys, how are you?

Richo: Gordon, your story is one that really captured our imaginations. You wrote a letter to Collingwood asking if you could have a game not when you were seven years of age, but when you were 27 years of age, and the even more remarkable thing is they wrote back and said yes!

Gordon Towan: Yes. Well, I did it. They actually said come down and have a run. And I did a full pre-season with the guys from October right through till March and then managed to play most of the pre-season games. We came to the last game and I played in the twos, I think the senior side were playing Norwood. And at the end of the game, myself and a couple of other guys got called into the office and were told 'Oh, thanks but no thanks'. So that was quite interesting.

Anyway, I said I'd like to know the reason I'm being cut and the official I asked said, 'You're too old'. And I said fair enough. At least I had a go. That sort of satisfied my need at that particular point.

Billy: But that wasn't the end, was it? You went back to Preston after that didn't you?

Gordon Towan: I played the previous three years or four seasons with Preston. And then in the '82 season we were having a pretty good year and then I got a call down to Collingwood halfway through the season, in May, which is a funny story in itself, because I nearly didn't go down there. Because as the process was going, I got a phone call from John Birt at work, and I was thinking to myself, this has got to be a mate of mine, a mate up in the bush named Pat Murphy. We used to play tricks on each other before each season started, or even during the season, where we used to ring up and say, 'Oh, I'm from some club, do you want to come and play with us?' And I thought he's gone another step this time because he's got someone else to ring up. So when John rang and he said he was from Collingwood, I thought 'Oh yeah', and he said, 'Would you like to come down and have a run?' And I said, 'Yeah, look, mate, I'll give you a ring back'. And I hung up. And it wasn't until about 20 minutes later, my wife rang up and said to me, who was the bloke from Collingwood that rang? And I sort of thought, oh, my mate wouldn't go that far. So I rang up the Preston secretary and he said, yeah, Collingwood is interested. Well, in about three seconds I reckon I was back on the phone to Birty and I said when do you want me down there mate! So I explained to him the situation as well with a funny story.

Billy: And why did they want you back?

Gordon Towan: I've got no idea. Well, I think Preston were playing pretty well. We had a pretty good side, those '81, '82, '83 teams. And '84. Pretty strong sides and Preston were on top of the ladder. Ray Shaw was captain-coach of the Preston side.

And yeah, we're playing pretty good football. And I suppose I was having a pretty good year '82. And I think it was helpful doing the pre-season with them the year before.

Richo: At this stage, you're 28 but Collingwood had played in the Grand Final the year before. And Round 9, you find yourself in the side. You did alright with your two games, one on the MCG one at Vic Park.

Gordon Towan: Yes that was fantastic. And it was a great opportunity. I don't know if I hold the record for actually being down there, I was down there six weeks. So talk about getting in and out.

Billy: Who was the was the coach of the Pies at the time?

Gordon Towan: Tommy Hafey was the coach when I went down there, I was down there when he got the sack.

Torch: So that was the year they brought Mickey Erwin in to take over wasn't it?

Gordon Towan: Yeah. And look, it was really fun. There were some funny stories after that. It was quite interesting going down there. I went down there and Hafey was on the highest pedestal from my point of view that you could have. I've come from Preston and getting the opportunity to actually play VFL football was fantastic. And seeing Hafey, he was like a god and you think, geez, this is fantastic. But I don't think he had the same level amongst a lot of the other players when I went down at that stage. And I think that was the result of how the team was playing, and they weren't playing that well, but look the opportunity there was fantastic.

Covey: Did you go right into the side after you got the phone call, you went in that week?

Gordon Towan: No, I went down there and I think Collingwood were playing the Swans. And I think it was the first year the Swans had moved to Sydney. I think there was talk that I was going to go straight in but I didn't, I went and played in the twos down at Lake Oval. So I played one game down there and then from there I was promoted to play against Hawthorn the following week.

Champs: What position? Half-back flank?

Gordon Towan: No, in the back pocket. I think Peter McCormack was full back at that stage, so I don't think I was going to take his spot.

Champs: Did you have to stand Leigh Matthews?

Gordon Towan: No, actually, it was quite interesting some of the players that were at Hawthorn that day. I think at one stage there I was on Gary Ablett. I think he came off the bench, I'm not sure, but he was good to play on. But the other one that sort of stuck in my mind was Gary Buckenara. And the game was so much faster from the level that I was used to. And at one stage in the third quarter, we were reasonably close and then Gary Buckenara pushed up to between centre-half-forward and the centre line. And I got caught up in the game, I started watching the game when it was down in our forward line, thinking 'how good is this!'. And then all of a sudden they got control of the ball in their back pocket and you know you get that sense that your player's not around you? And here's Buckenara, he must have been about 40 metres away from me on the half-forward line. So I took off but by the time I got there he's taken a mark, given me one on the way down and while I'm rolling around on the ground he goes back and kicks the goal. I thought 'Well, welcome to the VFL'.

Richo: And then Gordon your next and what turned out to be last game for Collingwood was at Vic Park against the Demons—who was your opponent that day?

Gordon Towan: Yeah, well, don't you have some memories! I ran on the field and I knew when I was going to the back pocket that some of the other guys had been given certain players to play on. So I've gone down to the back line just looking for someone to man up on and there's no one there, all the players were taken. So I'm looking around the field and I saw a player standing up on the square. And I thought I better go and pick this bloke up. And as I've run up to him, he's No. 2, Robbie Flower. And I think, you've got to be kidding me. I reckon in about five seconds, Peter Hafey, who was the runner, has come out and made a quick shift. Geez, that was funny, but I finished up playing on I think it was Dave McGlashan for Melbourne and then in the last half I played on Gerard Healy.

Champs: You've done alright for two games Gordon!

Billy: And what happened next week Gord?

Gordon Towan: Well, it was funny because the big story broke where Hafey got the sack on the Monday night. So we went down to training and back in the '80s, when you got there, training started at say five and you just turned up in those days and you got changed and you went out and had kick.

Torch: You had to run your two laps first!

Gordon Towan: Of course you had to do two laps. But this particular Tuesday night, Mick Erwin said no one's to go out. He said, right, we're all staying in, because there was a fairly hostile crowd outside at Vic Park after they put the big man Tommy Hafey off. It felt like there was about 4–5,000 people there and they were pretty angry. And anyway, we all got changed and we're running out and I don't know if you've been into the Vic Park change rooms but it is a bit of a tunnel that you go down and then you come up and run up onto the track. And as we're all going down as a team, as it worked out, Peter Moore was in front because he was the captain and he's working his way up the race but Ray Byrne was in between Peter and the rest of the team. And as Moorey's run up onto the track Byrney's turned around and stopped the rest of us, put his hands up and just pulled us all up. So Peter Moore has run out on the track and started running laps by himself, thinking there's a whole team behind him! You should have heard all the noise and the boos and then Moorey must have got about 30 or 40 metres and had this sense that there's no one there, he wasn't hearing any breathing. And he's turned around. Well, he's given us all a bit of a bake. And then we came out and we all copped it. But it was quite interesting. And then I think after that I just had a sense, there were five injuries in the backline. And I thought, If I get dropped, that'll be pretty much it for me. And sure enough, it did happen and for whatever reason there was six changes in that backline. I thought to myself, Well, I'll stay there for another couple of weeks to see what was going on. And then I had a talk with Preston and I thought, I'm 28, I've had my chance which was absolutely sensational and I could have stayed there the whole year, but I thought, I'm 28 and Collingwood's going to start to rebuild. Well, you might as well give some young kid an opportunity to come up rather than keeping some crusty old bugger down there.

Covey: And sadly 4–5,000 people didn't turn up to the protest your exit.

Torch: At the end of that year, how did the Bullants go? Did you win the Premiership?

Gordon Towan: No, we got into the Grand Final which was great but Port beat us by seven points. But the following year we did and that was fantastic. So I've achieved the goals I wanted to, which is great.

Richo: Tremendous Gordon, thank you so much for your time.

Gordon Towan: Not a problem. A great pleasure. And thanks for having me on guys.

Richo: All the very best. Gordon Towan, two games for Collingwood at age 28 in 1982.

BLOODY BYRNE!
Boo!
Boo!
MAGPIES
BRING BACK TOMMY
Boo!
TOMMY!
PIES
YOU CAN'T TOUCH HIM!
Ptooi!

Sydney's Swans

RICKY QUADE

Ricky Quade was an in-and-under midfielder for South Melbourne who became the inaugural coach of the relocated Sydney Swans for the 1982 season. It was a tough road to travel—the decision to move the team was hotly opposed by many South supporters—and after two and a half years, Ricky was done. But he wasn't sacked, his body was telling him not to go on.

Richo: Ricky Quade, welcome to the Coodabeens.

Ricky Quade: Good morning fellas.

Billy: Ricky, what happened there in mid-1984?

Ricky Quade: We were going along pretty well then the wheels fell off a bit and I ended up with a burst ulcer and in hospital for 10 days and that was it. Tony Franklin took over for one game and then Bob Hammond came in before John Northey.

Richo: That was a big shock at the time because everyone was saying 'Bob Who?' And of course, not Bob who to anyone in South Australia, he's a legend of South Australian footy. But it seemed the most unlikely appointment at the time, do you know how that came about?

Ricky Quade: I'm not sure but while he wasn't a household name in Sydney, not too many VFL people were at the time, to be honest. Bob did a terrific job because it was a difficult time. The club was nearly on its knees again and Bob really straightened the place out and filled in until John Northey came along and he did a great job.

Covey: Ricky, we remember you as one of the real tough players, hard at the ball and played with injuries and that sort of stuff. But a burst ulcer—was that as painful a thing that you had happened to you? How did it rate in the footy injury scale?

Ricky Quade: It was not the best, not at my age anyway and it sort of crept up on me, but according to the doctors it was the result of a pretty stressful time. All the acrimony around the '82 move and the friendships lost as a result of that were pretty difficult for quite a few people. At that time the Sydney people didn't want us to win, they wanted us to get back to Melbourne as quickly as possible and the people in Melbourne didn't want us to win so we were a bit of a lost soul there for a while. And I think that may have taken its toll and it could have been done a lot better, the whole thing looking back on it.

Covey: While it was a stressful time and all, there were the occasional relaxing moments such as the party at Lady Fairfax's. We've spoken to several former players who went along, like Tony Morwood and others, and they quite enjoyed the occasion. Can you recall much about wining and dining?

Ricky Quade: Well, that's interesting, because all the celebrities were allowed inside but the players were all outside. I went into the house to use the toilet and I got kicked out, that really sort of summed up the social set in Sydney. I think Roundy and a few of the fellas like Browning and Morwood and those blokes just sat underneath a tree and drank all their grog.

Covey: You stayed living in Sydney and I trust you're allowed into a few more houses these days.

Ricky Quade: I hope so but we didn't have much money in those days so the boys may have taken a few souvenirs.

Billy: Ricky having been under the microscope and being a high-profile Melbourne identity, it must have been a lovely change when you got up there and could be anonymous in Sydney.

Ricky Quade: We were until people found out who we were. I can remember waking up one morning in our second year because in the first year we just flew in and there's a guy on the radio named Ron Casey. Not our Ron Casey but 'Won' Casey. And he was going on about he wished these carpetbaggers would just get back to Melbourne, so that was a pretty good welcome for us. But we gradually won the people over and we're sitting here, a pretty important ingredient of the sporting landscape up here at the moment.

Covey: Ricky, one of our regular members, Torch McGee, is not with us today because he's on holidays but Torchy's an old South man, and he's always telling us they have reunions all the time. Have you managed to join in and catch up with all the South boys?

Ricky Quade: Yeah, I do but I think if I went to every one I'd be an alcoholic. They seem to like the social side of things the old South Melbourne people. Those were tremendous days and the '96 Grand Final really united the old South Melbourne supporters and the Sydney supporters and really brought them together, and Richard Colless did an absolutely marvellous job in engineering all that, it was just fantastic.

Champs: And, Ricky, your views on the arrival of Western Sydney?

Ricky Quade: Certainly if you had've said it to me even five years ago, I wouldn't have thought that would have happened. And they've got their knockers up here but I think on the field, perhaps apart from last week, they've been very competitive. They play a style not dissimilar to the Swans actually, a pretty combative style. I think it's taken its toll a little bit on the younger bodies. But the AFL do things pretty well these days, and they didn't go into it lightly and Kevin Sheedy is a tremendous appointment, he's really been well received up here. I'm not quite sure if they understand half of his smart aleck remarks. It will certainly take time, there's no question about that but I think they've got a tremendous young list and they're well coached and they'll do well eventually.

Champs: Well, it's certainly being managed a lot better than what you had to go through 30 years ago, there's no doubt about that.

Ricky Quade: We're all wise in hindsight, but it could have been done a lot better. If we had just been given the resources it wasn't so much even the money side or the playing side of it, it was just that there were absolutely no facilities—no training facilities, no gymnasiums, no dressing rooms. You just have to look at what's available today and we're not envious, but thank God it has come such a long way.

Billy: Having had your coaching career end so abruptly in 1984, did you harbour any ambitions or thoughts about wanting to coach again?

Ricky Quade: No, not really though I guess I missed that intimate involvement. I was fortunate enough after a couple of years to go back as chairman of selectors and I was on the board for about 14 years. Actually, I was only going to go on for two but Richard Colless is a pretty persuasive guy, he said just go on for two and that'll be it, but I was still there 14 years later. So look, it's been terrific to be involved from that side of it and I really did enjoy that and they are a terrific club to be involved with.

Richo: And Ricky there's also no doubt about it, that when you go to a game at the Sydney Cricket Ground, it really feels like a footy game. It's not like going to the footy in Melbourne, but it's the real deal and the Sydney supporters are right into it.

Ricky Quade: Yeah, they really are. And it just creates a tremendous atmosphere at the ground. We've got a really hardcore 20–25,000 members there and they certainly get into it and they know what their football is about now. They may have struggled when we first went up there with the rules but now that they're really into it, it's a great atmosphere. It's a smaller type ground, it's a bit more like some of the old suburban grounds with some of the stands there, but it's a great spot.

Richo: It's now an unqualified success and you go back to how hard it was that it gave you an ulcer, but you are just an indispensable part of a great piece of football history, Ricky.

Ricky Quade: Thanks very much for that. But there were a lot of people involved as I said before. What Richard Colless did pulling that club together, because when he came it was really a basket case and that was the last shot at it. And getting Ron Barassi involved—Barassi did a marvellous job, he really had everything to lose and nothing to gain by coming up here at the time. He and Richard really took it back to basics and they recruited people like Tony Lockett and Paul Roos and they made it a membership-based club and got it up and running and it is what it is today.

Richo: And here they go, they look like playing finals again. Ricky it has been wonderful talking to you this morning. Thanks so much.

Ricky Quade: Thanks very much for the time fellas.

Richo: Ricky Quade, inaugural coach of the Sydney Swans when South Melbourne moved up to Sydney in 1982. And the number of times people look across to the coach's box and say, oh gee, that bloke will be bursting an ulcer, well it actually happened to Ricky Quade!

BOB HAMMOND

When Ricky Quade dramatically departed the coaching box in 1984, the Swans called on South Australia's Bob Hammond to replace him. Virtually unknown to VFL fans, Hammond was a legend of the SANFL and stepped in for the remaining eight games of the season.

Richo: Welcome to the Coodabeens, Bob.

Bob Hammond: Morning, gentlemen.

Richo: Tell us how it came about that the finger of fate pointed to you to step in as the midseason replacement at the Sydney Swans all the way from Adelaide.

Bob Hammond: I guess watching the Swans on Sundays was a ritual for me as it was for most football-interested people. So, I watched the Swans this particular Sunday and I can't tell you the result but it was great day's entertainment and lo and behold, on the Monday, I get a phone call from Alan Schwab who, in essence, said we'd like you to coach the Swans and I thought it was a prank. He said I'm coming over to talk to you which he and Greg Miller duly did on the Monday. I guess there's a little bit of background necessary. I'd coached in the SANFL for six years with Norwood and I'd retired from that because of the business commitments I had. And

I was still coach of the South Australian state side which had beaten Victoria in the State of Origin in that year. And I knew Alan Schwab from the Mike Patterson days—Mike had come to North Adelaide and coached us and he was ex-Richmond—and Alan and Greg Miller came to Adelaide and said we'd like to see the remainder of the season out and we'd like to talk to you at the end of the season about going on. Anyway, cutting a long story short, that was on the Monday. I made a decision on the Tuesday to do it. I flew to Melbourne on the Wednesday, went up and conducted training on the Thursday night and we played Fitzroy at the Junction Oval on the Saturday.

Richo: And you got a win first up.

Bob Hammond: Yes, we had a win.

Richo: Bob, you did mention your coaching career prior to the Swans included coaching Norwood to Premierships in '75 and '78. One of Norwood's biggest fans, Greg Champion is here to talk to you.

Bob Hammond: One of my great mates, Greg.

Champs: Good on you, Bob. Thanks for all those Norwood flags! And Bob, before the Norwood flags you had a decorated career as a North Adelaide full back?

Bob Hammond: Yeah, I played 230 or 240 games for North Adelaide.

Champs: And stepped into a Premiership side in your very first senior season.

Bob Hammond: In 1960, yes, and we were also successful in '71 and '72 as far as Premierships are concerned.

Billy: Bob, I'm curious, you were a decorated player at North Adelaide. You were the captain in '73. But 1974 finds you the captain of Norwood. How did that all come about?

Bob Hammond: Well, in the middle of my footy career with

North Adelaide, I had two years of footy in Port Pirie as captain of a side called Ports. Business had taken me there, I was with Dunlop in those days and this was my first management appointment. And, so, I was playing coach there. So, I suppose in some respects, the Norwood appointment had something to do with that experience. I had none at league level but had a couple of years in the bush where we were successful, so I presume that had something to do with their selection.

Richo: Yeah, that's right. Jumping in at Port Pirie is just like jumping into Sydney. I imagine the accommodation and everything once you arrived in Sydney was rather different to Port Pirie.

Bob Hammond: Slightly different, yes. They've got a sort of a coat hanger up there that's a bit bigger than anything in Port Pirie.

Billy: Did you chat to Ricky Quade at all? Did you give Ricky a bell?

Bob Hammond: No, I didn't know because I jumped in at the deep end. Dean Moore who is the football manager there now was the football manager at the time. So, on the Thursday night, I had Dean walk around one metre behind me and whispering in my ear the names of the individuals because I only knew about six or seven, so I'd just turn my head and Dean would say that's Paul Hawke, or whoever it may have been. And, on the lighter side of things, I had them sit in the change room in their respective position so that I could get their names right because I had a board up behind them with their names on it. And it was going alright until three-quarter time and one of the selectors, it might have been Tony Franklin, said 'Let's change Christmas with Tilt', and I had no idea what he was talking about! But it was, of course, Wayne Carroll and Rod Carter.

Billy: How did the players relate to you, Bob, did they make it easy for you?

Bob Hammond: Yes, they did, they were fantastic. In fact, you've got to realise that there was a group of young men, with families in some instances, just wanting to apply their craft and get on as far as playing football is concerned. They weren't interested in politics or anything of that nature but they were more than welcoming to me. I really formed some strong relationships as far as those guys were concerned and we had a good 8–10 weeks, whatever it might have been, and the respect that they showed me I'll never forget.

Torch: Now one of the players you had there, of course, was a fella named Warwick Capper. How did you get on with the Wiz?

Bob Hammond: Well, I gave Warwick his first game, so don't hold that against me! He was a young, young man in those days just wanting to play football. And we gave him the opportunity and the rest is history.

Champs: And how close were you to going on and coaching them the next year, Bob?

Bob Hammond: It was never really a possibility. I mean, I was there A, to help out, and B, for the wonderful experience that it turned out to be but I did have three supermarkets here in Adelaide and they were the priority at that stage.

Billy: Champs, did you used to shop at Bob Hammond's supermarkets?

Champs: I was too young! Bobby, looking back at your career, you played in the South Australian side when they won in Melbourne in '63?

Bob Hammond: Yes, I was only 21, that was my first state game and I stood Doug Wade. And I think it was the first time South Australia had beaten Victoria in something like 50 years but don't quote me on that.

Champs: That was the 1963 game at the 'G but in '83, when you coached South Australia to a win over Victoria, was that at Footy Park?

Bob Hammond: Yes, it was yes.

Champs: And you hadn't won too often against the Vics at any time.

Bob Hammond: Our record in State of Origin is not bad. But against Victoria the record's not so good.

Richo: And Bob, that '63 game is historic in many ways because the rules were changed. It was after that game that having a huddle at quarter-time was introduced. Up until that point the teams had just swapped over. But Bobby Davis said that if only he'd been able to talk to the Vics at quarter-time...

Bob Hammond: We would have won by more!

Champs: Back at North Adelaide, Bob, and winning flags in '60, '71 and '72, North haven't had a hell of a lot of glory since those glory days.

Bob Hammond: I think they've won one flag since then. But, no, they've struggled a bit unfortunately. They're in good hands now with Bohdan Jaworski who played in the same side as I did and he's the president. I think they're making some strides at the moment.

Champs: Were you on the AFL commission until last year?

Bob Hammond: Yes, I resigned in October after 11 years.

Richo: Well, now that you're not on the commission, Bob, you can tell us what you really think.

Bob Hammond: I think the AFL is a wonderful institution and it should be respected.

Champs: It's been during the last decade that there's been so much change including the introduction of Gold Coast and Greater Western Sydney. It's been remarkable period.

Bob Hammond: Well, it has been a remarkable period, and as

Greg will tell you it was also a remarkable experience for all of us with introduction of the Crows 20 years ago.

Billy: Bob, you've seen a lot of football, who's the best pound for pound footballer you've seen in any state in your association with football?

Bob Hammond: Clearly Barrie Robran.

Torch: No hesitation there.

Bob Hammond: I've got to admit some bias here because I played probably 200 games with him and I got to see him week in, week out on display. But I maintain that he is the best I've seen and I've seen nothing to change my mind.

Billy: And he's an absolute gentleman.

Bob Hammond: Yes, he's a fantastic guy.

Richo: Bob, it's been tremendous talking to you. Thank you so much.

Bob Hammond: My pleasure. Cheers.

Richo: Bob Hammond there, an absolute giant of Australian football. Bob, of course, was the inaugural chairman of the Crows. He did 10 years as chairman of Adelaide and then went to the commission for 10 years. And in those first 10 years the door was always open to you when Bob was there, wasn't it Greg?

Champs: It's all changed now!

Richo: I can just imagine you wheeling your trolley through one of Bob's supermarkets and loading up with Woody's lemonade and Southwark.

Champs: And Bobby would have been on the checkout, too!

Bob Hammond died in 2020 after a battle with Parkinson's Disease.

BERNIE CONLEN

South Melbourne's relocation to Sydney has been a recurring theme over the years probably due to the fact that things blew up in 1981—our first year on-air. And the party at Lady Fairfax's harbourside mansion gets mentioned nearly as often as the Peanut Man. Bernie Conlen, one of our Two Game Wonders, was in the thick of it as a fledgling Swan. He left the Lakeside nest and flew west to the SANFL where he lives almost 40 years later.

Richo: Bernie joins us from Alberton where he is watching West Adelaide play Port Adelaide. Bernie Conlen, welcome to the Coodabeens.

Bernie Conlen: Good morning fellas, it's such a pleasure to be on.

Richo: Before we get you to tell us about your two games, tell us about what the atmosphere was like amongst the players and everybody around the club when the Sydney thing exploded suddenly at the end of the '81 season?

Bernie Conlen: Yeah, well, it sort of exploded halfway through. It sort of gently came through to us that we were going to move and then we had the Keep South at South Committee and one board was sacked and they brought in Bill Collins, The Accurate One, to become our president. The coach then became John Rantall after Stewy resigned, or retired I think more accurately. And he had also had an assistant coach in Peter Bedford. So that that was like an interim measure over the season until eventually the VFL said, no you're going to Sydney, the votes have come in and we went off and then the board was put off, the coach was sacked and Ricky Quade took over as the inaugural Sydney coach.

Richo: And there you were, a 163cm kid from Oakleigh, just trying to get a game.

Bernie Conlen: That's right and struggling pretty hard to get a game, too, I might add.

Covey: Did you just have the one year there, Bernie?

Bernie Conlen: No, I started off in about August '79. I went down there and did their pre-season and stayed until the end of '82.

Richo: So you had a year up in Sydney?

Bernie Conlen: Well, we didn't actually move to Sydney. I think Bernie Evans and Colin Hounsell or Mark Browning were the only players actually based in Sydney, the rest of us would fly up to each home game in Sydney. And then the following year, in '83, we were expected to move up and that's when I parted company because I thought for me going up there, I would still struggle for a game so I came over here to Adelaide.

Torch: Did you originally come from Oakleigh in the VFA? Or were you an Oakleigh Districts boy?

Bernie Conlen: No, Oakleigh Districts. I started my junior career at Notting Hill. They only had juniors that went to Under 17s. And then when that ran out, I went to Oakleigh Districts Under 18s and senior football from the Under 18s.

Torch: There must have been about four of you from Oakleigh Districts playing at South at that time?

Bernie Conlen: Warwick Capper was in the Under 19s at that

stage. But there was Michael Wright, Steven Wright, the Wright brothers. David Winbanks played a few years later. And David Rhys-Jones, too.

Richo: You were all zoned were you, Bernie, back then?

Bernie Conlen: Yep, I was on the cusp, I was in South Melbourne's zone, but if I moved across the road, I was in Richmond territory.

Covey: And for listeners to the program, including our producer who wasn't born in 1981, we should point out that Conlen is spelt with an E, so you're no relation to Mickey Conlan.

Bernie Conlen: Correct, though I did once get pulled over by a cop in Melbourne and he was a Fitzroy supporter. Mickey Conlan soon became my brother there, but definitely no relation.

Covey: And you didn't quite have Mickey's build.

Bernie Conlen: No, well, I thought I did, but the statue is a little bit shorter and a little bit thinner.

Covey: It must have been a big thrill after you played all of 1980 and most of '81 in the reserves to finally get picked to make your debut in Round 21.

Bernie Conlen: It was very gratifying. I felt a lot of gratitude towards Ian Stewart. I think he gave it as a reward. I was a fairly fierce trainer and he came to me on the Thursday night and said, 'Son, I'm going to give you a treat, you're in the ones tonight'. So that was a big thrill. I've still got fond memories. And my time at South Melbourne, and the first year of the Sydney Swans, they were a great bunch of people and I thoroughly enjoyed it.

Covey: So you played in that game against Essendon. Did Stewie tell you you're in for the last two games or just the one and then you got picked again?

Bernie Conlen: I got picked again. I was picked on the bench for Essendon but he roved two rovers out of the pocket so he had Silvio Foschini on one side and he was picked up by Shane Heard, I believe. And I got stood by Neale Daniher which was a big thrill.

Billy: They picked you again next week when South played North Melbourne which must have been a thrill as well. You must have been dirty though that you never played against Melbourne because you would have towelled up Paul Callery. You had him covered at 163cm!

Bernie Conlen: Well, he actually ended up at South Melbourne for a short time there in 1980. It was quite pleasing to have him there especially when we would do hamstring stretches and I thought my legs were short!

Champs: I want to talk about your career in Adelaide, Bernie. You went to West and you played in a Premiership and you're still involved in local football?

Bernie Conlen: Yeah, just the past players, we have an enormous past players group at West Adelaide, one of the strongest in the league. And you know, we have Wednesday night raffles down at the club, and each week we have a past player as a special guest speaker. I don't know if you boys would know Freddy Bills, he played for West Torrens. And we had him last week and some of the stories he told were absolutely brilliant. It's a great atmosphere. I enjoy being involved.

Covey: And what's the raffle prize Bernie, a nice red from the Barossa or something?

Bernie Conlen: We sometimes sneak a red in there but it's a side of lamb. I've got about three sides of lamb so there are a few lopsided sheep around!

Richo: They're traditional values, Bernie. And you're on the line to us from Alberton as we speak?

Bernie Conlen: That's correct, it's a beautiful day here and if anyone's coming down, I'd bring a crocheted rug because it's a bit chilly.

Billy: And you are playing Port Adelaide. Have you got the car locked up and the GPS hidden under a blanket or something Bernie?

Bernie Conlen: Actually I bring the bricks down and put the car up on bricks, they won't go near it then.

Covey: Do you still keep an eye on the Swans?

Bernie Conlen: I do but I'm actually a Kangaroos supporter, I've followed them most of my life. But certainly I have a sentimental spot for the Swans and they're doing alright. A lot of people have written them off this year but they're always around the mark under Roosy, he's quite a good coach.

Covey: Given you have been in Adelaide now for some time, earlier today we were talking about the Jack Oatey Medal and the Fos Williams Medal and apparently only one player has won both. And he won two Fos Williams Medals in '84 and '88 and a Jack Oatey in '85. Who was it, Bernie?

Bernie Conlen: It wasn't Garry McIntosh?

Covey: No, we're talking an all-time South Australian legend who went to play in Melbourne, still involved with one of the AFL clubs. Stephen Kernahan! Did you play against him?

Bernie Conlen: I certainly did. In '83, I actually ran third in the Magarey Medal but by the records it says that I was runner-up because young Stephen Kernahan won it with 44 votes. And the next nearest person to him was Tony Antrobus and he was awarded the Magarey because Kernas has given a love tap slap across someone's face, it was the softest tap you're ever going to see and he was rubbed out and didn't receive the medal. I remember at the count, Steve's father Harry had his head in his hands all night, he didn't look up once, it was the saddest sight.

Covey: And the votes just kept on coming in.

Bernie Conlen: They were pouring in, he was the most outstanding footballer for the year and he couldn't get the just desserts of the medal.

Champs: And you can imagine Neil Kerley thinking if you're gonna get disqualified, you might as well make it worthwhile!

Richo: Bernie, thanks for talking to us today and enjoy the rest of your day there at Alberton and watching your beloved West Adelaide go around. Are they gonna win?

Bernie Conlen: They should do. The reserves are four goals up at the moment and the boys are just starting to get their act together. We're not expecting to take the flag but we are a lot more competitive this year.

Richo: So you expect to knock them off?

Bernie Conlen: I think so.

Richo: Bernie, terrific. Have a great day today.
Bernie Conlen played two games for South Melbourne in 1981. In what was, at the time, one of the most tumultuous periods of footy that we've ever seen.

JAMIE SIDDONS

Jamie Siddons is well known as a prolific scorer of first class runs for Victoria and South Australia over three decades and he is also one of the unluckiest cricketers never to play for Australia. But what you may not be aware of is that Jamie was also a champion footballer who played the game at the highest level. Jamie Siddons joined us from Bangladesh, where he was coaching the national cricket team, in 2009.

Richo: Jamie Siddons, welcome to the Coodabeen Champions. Now you played two games for the Sydney Swans in 1984. How long had you been on the list before you finally got games in the ones?

Jamie Siddons: I don't know, eight or 10 weeks.

Torch: Where were you actually recruited from Jamie?

Jamie Siddons: Robinvale.

Torch: So you weren't in the Swan's traditional New South Wales zone?

Jamie Siddons: No.

Richo: And at that stage, had you decided whether cricket or footy was going to be it?

Jamie Siddons: No, I was just enjoying sport, I was a country boy just playing both sports, summer and winter. And I think I'd played with the Vic Second XI that year and thought cricket was it. Then I got to play with the Swans and I thought football might be it but I took cricket in the end.

Billy: Were your two games in a row, Jamie?

Jamie Siddons: Yes, one was at the MCG and the next one was in Sydney and then the next week, I had a crook back and got a few injections and didn't like that so I took off home I think after a week.

Billy: What number did you wear?

Jamie Siddons: 50.

Billy: Gee, you got your half ton up in your first game!

Richo: And you kicked the one goal.

Jamie Siddons: I kicked one, it was a scrubber too, I remember Barry Mitchell handballed it to me and I munged it through. I was about 20 metres out.

Torch: At that time, 1984, it was a pretty exciting time up at the Swans. Was Dr. Edelsten in charge by that time?

Jamie Siddons: Yeah, he was there. I was training in Melbourne at the Albert Ground and travelled to Sydney for a couple of weeks to meet a few blokes and train there and then play, but half the squad was still in Melbourne, Warwick Capper I think was still in Melbourne as well. So it was funny, not meeting your teammates and then playing with them was a bit strange.

Champs: Robinvale being in the corner of three states you've had connections to all three states—South Australia, Victoria and New South Wales, did you play football when you went back to Robinvale with your crook back?

Jamie Siddons: I didn't play that year because I'd signed and played with Sydney so I couldn't go back and play with the boys. But the next year I played a few games. Actually, I think I played one game and then got a phone call from Cricket Australia to say did I want to come and play some other games with them.

Champs: And you said, nah I can't, we're playing Merbein this week.

Jamie Siddons: That's what it was at the Swans because the night games were played on a Tuesday and I played a couple of those first. So I'd play those on a Tuesday and go back and play for Robinvale on a Saturday.

Billy: Jamie, you're over there in Dakar at the moment, tell us a bit about life in Bangladesh, and your work coaching the national cricket team.

Jamie Siddons: Well, it's interesting, every day is a new day and very exciting but it's a very poor country, very poverty ridden country and a little bit corrupt. I love the people, the people are fantastic. My cricket team are very young. When I first got here, I made some big decisions on some older players and pushed them aside and took on some players that I thought could develop. The infrastructure is pretty poor and the players weren't quite ready for international cricket so we're copping a few smackings but I've seen big improvements over the last few years. Last month we beat Sri Lanka and New Zealand in one day cricket so we're moving forward.

Richo: And Jamie how does this system work for talent identification? How do you and your colleagues pick out the likely younger players coming on?

Jamie Siddons: We've got a national competition here and we've also got a very good club one day competition which is taking place at the moment so that's probably the main way. But the hard part is getting the youth through because there's no real cricket out in the other areas. The main cricket is played in Dakar which is the capital and the infrastructure out in the broader areas is not good. There's 150 million people here and most of them love and play cricket but it's hard to find the talent and develop it.

Champs: And your time in South Australia, Jamie, I imagine you had a happy time there and did you ever play a footy game in Adelaide?

Jamie Siddons: No. I moved there after Victoria won the Shield as a 26-year-old and I didn't play a game of football after 21 I don't think.

Champs: But you had a good time in Adelaide?

Jamie Siddons: I love Adelaide, I loved living there and I loved playing cricket for South Australia. It was a good time, we took a young side through to win a Shield and haven't won one since. I don't know what happened with them, they've got a good team in now, they've played some pretty good cricket towards the end of this year.

Champs: Do you know what nationality you feel because you come from right on the border there at Robinvale.

Jamie Siddons: I'm definitely Victorian but as far as my cricket I've spent, I think, nine years in South Australia and six or seven first class years in Victoria. I'm not too sure, maybe neither of them want me back!

Richo: You're very much wanted where you are on an absolute adventure being a national cricket coach of the Bangladesh cricket team. Jamie, do you keep your eye on the footy at all?

Jamie Siddons: I love the footy, Hawthorn is my team so when they made the Grand Final, I went down to the Australian embassy and watched the whole game and went to a glitter ball and went dressed as a Hawthorn Premiership player.

Richo: And your old team the Swans have got the Hawks this weekend.

Jamie Siddons: I think I'll still be going for the Hawks, we need to get a win on the board. Maybe the Swans do too I'm not sure what happened with them last week.

Richo: They need one as well. Jamie, I'm sure you'll be able to follow the game via ABC's *Grandstand* on the internet. Enjoy the rest of your day, and thanks for joining us.

Jamie Siddons: Thanks guys.

Say Hi To Your Mum For Us

JANE WINES

By the end of our conversation with Jane Wines, mum of Port Power star Ollie, we had some pretty detailed instructions on the best driving route from Echuca to Adelaide. We spoke to Jane in the pre-finals bye weekend in 2017 as she and husband Tony were getting a few things done around the house before heading over to Adelaide for Port's finals campaign.

Richo: Good morning, Jane.

Jane Wines: Hello, how are you? Firstly, can I say I'm very flattered to be asked to come on as a mum, because I thought my expiry time was up. No, he'll always be mine and I'm his mum but in the football world I thought oh, they've had enough of me, they're sick of me, so thank you.

Covey: We've never heard you speak before, Jane, so we couldn't be sick of you.

Richo: Where are you speaking to us from this morning?

Jane Wines: We are from Echuca on the Murray River, 3564.

Covey: It's a long way to go to watch Ollie play.

Jane Wines: It is but sometimes we prefer to drive because the airport from here is probably two hours to Tullamarine and then you've got a 57-minute flight, depending on the wind, to Adelaide. But, in fact, we love driving and we go up and across the Mallee and it's a really nice drive.

Richo: Tell us about draft night because obviously you'd known for some time that he was a good player, he was going to be drafted and he could go anywhere. But how well do you remember that night and his name coming up?

Jane Wines: I probably remember it a lot better than my husband. We didn't know he was going to Port Adelaide, they didn't interview him so we hadn't met any of them. That was because they didn't think he'd get through to them at No. 7 and take that for what it is, you know, that's what happened. My husband Tony was quite green, they phoned him the day before to say that if he was there, they would be taking him. I had to kind of go on Tony's look and what he was feeling and on draft night it's all a blur, you're just worried about them. But we are so thrilled, he's got two sisters and a brother and we were all there together and Port Adelaide was magnificent.

Champs: How did Ollie feel about going to Port?

Jane Wines: I'll be brutally honest, he was a bit shocked. But then I don't know any different, he could have been shocked to know that he was going anywhere, we'll never know. But look, honestly, I said the first year, I didn't even know there was a place called Alberton.

Richo: You were saying though that the Port Adelaide people were terrific.

Jane Wines: They've just been fantastic, it's like a big country club, it's very similar to Echuca but it's on a much bigger scale, of course. But it's just that kind of feeling when you get there, the supporters are brilliant, they're very, very honest and they're very funny. And we've had to learn a lot about football in Adelaide, don't you worry about that.

ECHUCA
CHINA
LAKE BOGA
SEA LAKE
WAIPEUP
OLLIE'S TROLLEY
PINARA
SPEED
SLOW DOWN
TAILEM BEND
EAGLE ON THE HILL
ADELAIDE
ALBERTON
HARV

Covey: Jane, have you met Kochie? And what's he like?

Jane Wines: I love Kochie. We know Kochie quite well, I think everyone at the club knows Kochie.

Billy: I bet he doesn't drive through the Mallee to get to the games.

Jane Wines: You never know with Kochie, he's a surprise package. He actually grabbed his family and threw them in a Winnebago the first year that Ollie was at Port Adelaide and they landed in Moama.

Richo: Just over the river from you.

Jane Wines: He's brilliant, but the people you meet and the opportunities and they're all good people. I mean, there's some bad people as you know in that industry that are a little bit ooh...

Covey: Allegedly.

Jane Wines: Can I tell you that there is one person who is connected with Port and I'm trying to get her into this region to put some money in here. Gina Rinehart's connected to Port now and that's my next really hard get.

Richo: I wouldn't have thought she'd be an Alberton-type person.

Jane Wines: Through Shanghai, through the Chinese connection.

Covey: Don't give too much away, Jane!

Champs: Does Gina throw the family in the Winnebago?

Jane Wines: I don't think so!

Covey: Did you go to the game in China, Jane?

Jane Wines: We sure did. That was the highlight, it was just overwhelming to see him run out in Shanghai to play football. Other than his first game ever, which was the highlight, the first game he played, this was the second most emotional day for me. It was really special over there and we went and we had a great time. There were about 15 parents and we really enjoyed the whole experience.

Covey: I presume your son was named Oliver. When did he become Ollie?

Jane Wines: I think he became Ollie pretty quickly, when he was in his little bassinet, they used to call it Ollie's Trolley and they'd wheel it out and go 'Here's Ollie in his trolley'. I think that's where it all started and I did get a little bit sad because now they put him down as Ollie Wines, he's technically in the record as Ollie Wines.

Covey: He's got to go through his John Farnham moment and change from Ollie back to Oliver.

Jane Wines: One day I hope Oliver Wines is on the door or on his badge when he's flying for Qantas. Captain Oliver Wines, that'd be nice.

Torch: And who did he barrack for when he was a young fella?

Jane Wines: He was a little Carlton supporter.

Covey: What about you and Tony?

Jane Wines: You can probably gather that I love sport and we fight about who our kids get their talents from as all parents do. But I wasn't right into footy, I used to love watching it, so I would follow whoever was actually winning that year, I'd pick them up, but that's all changed, don't worry. Tony's always been torn between probably Carlton and Geelong.

Champs: How has Ollie settled in to Adelaide? Is he partnered up or does he live with other players?

Jane Wines: Well, that's where I thought this is really funny you asking me. He hasn't got a partner and once they get a partner or wife, I've noticed that the mum falls off, she goes down the pecking order. I no longer have access to the coach, he won't take my calls, why is that after five years? It used to be like the Batphone, he picked it up because they wanted to look after you, which they still do. But he has settled really well in Adelaide, he had to make friends so a lot of his friends are the footballers, but that's really good. He lives with two other players. Tommy Clurey and Darcy Byrne-Jones.

Covey: I get the impression that you and Tony have brought him up very well over the years and maybe at some stage you listened to the Coodabeens years ago and introduced him to us because Ollie has tweeted at us occasionally in the last couple of years.

Jane Wines: Has he? Well, Tony's so jealous, when I said they're going to phone me and they want to speak to me, he said 'I think they've got it wrong, do they know that it's Father's Day?'

Richo: Well, hello, Tony and you have a good day tomorrow but, no, we're talking to Jane. When will you be hopping in the car and driving over to Adelaide?

Jane Wines: We've had a really good break in Echuca doing some spring cleaning because when the footy season's on you don't get a lot done around the house. But we'll head across the Mallee, we're not flying, we'll take the car and we'll drive on Friday morning.

Champs: What route do you take Jane? Talk us through Echuca to Adelaide.

Jane Wines: Well, we've got the best route, we have got such an amazing track. We go to Lake Boga then we cut across and I think that's where I've heard your show because on some of those trips Tony listens to you. So I've had to listen to you and I've actually really enjoyed it. We go Lake Boga then we cut across to Sea Lake, then you go to all those funny little towns like Speed, can you believe there's a town called Speed?

Richo: And the sign that says Speed, please slow down.

Jane Wines: And then the silo place where all the enormous artwork is, we just turn right before then and we end up in Walpeup. Then from Walpeup, that's when you're heading into real South Australian little towns like Pinaroo and Lamaroo, we love it.

Richo: At what stage do you actually join a major highway?

Jane Wines: Well, it's a small one at Walpeup. Then you hit the big one at Tailem Bend.

Richo: And then before you know it, you're at the Eagle on the Hill and you're heading down into Adelaide.

Jane Wines: We love the Eagle on the Hill and then we head down and we go left and down to Henley or Glenelg we go.

Covey: It's a long trip and the Port Adelaide scarf will be out the window all the way from Echuca. Good luck Jane!

Jane Wines: Thank you!

SHELLEY HAYNES

Grand Final day is always a big day with our annual OB (outside broadcast) on the concourse at the MCG. It was an even bigger day for the GWS Giants in 2019 when they reached their first Grand Final against Richmond. The Giants won their way into the decider by outlasting Collingwood in an exhausting, rain-soaked battle a week earlier. An interview with players' parents is a feature of the OB and joining us this day was Shelley Haynes, mother of GWS star Nick Haynes.

Richo: Hello again, Shelley. When did we last speak to you?

Shelley Haynes: That was two years ago and I had flown from Darwin to Sydney on a 6am flight. You got me early.

Covey: And that was to go and watch Nick play, wasn't it?

Shelley Haynes: Yeah, it was in the final that day against West Coast.

Richo: Shelley, tell us about Nick's footy background. He was drafted in the first GWS draft, which was 2011, where had he been playing his footy before then?

Shelley Haynes: He played his junior football in Somerville down past Frankston until he was about 12 or 13 and then he went to Frankston Rovers, then he had a break from footy for three or four years after he broke his arm and decided to go off and do other things like...

Champs: He had three or four years off as a teenager?

Shelley Haynes: Yes, he didn't go back, he went skimboarding and doing all those things down at Frankston foreshore and then his mate said, can you come back and play in the Under 18s, we need a player, so he went and played for Frankston Bombers in Under 18s.

Richo: He must've played pretty well then to be elevated to the TAC?

Shelley Haynes: He didn't straight away, he played another year at the Frankston Bombers senior team as an Under 18, then he went to the Stingrays as a 19-year-old as an over-ager, so he did alright. And that Grand Final he kicked three goals but the recruiters thought he kicked six but that's okay, we'll take that.

Billy: Shelley, what's the family background? Are you all sporty people?

Shelley Haynes: I have a netball background, I played netball at a fairly high level and his dad was a good footballer from Bendigo, he played at Golden Square with Greg Williams and the like.

Richo: So, the whole thing of the TAC squad and the possibility of getting drafted was something you were all fairly fluent with?

Shelley Haynes: It wasn't in Nick's mind, the Stingrays invited him along with 70 other kids to that day and we had to actually drag him along to that. He never thinks he's good enough but we recognised that he had some talent so we basically had to push him out the door and say get out there and show yourself and he did go on to win the Stingrays' best and fairest.

Torch: When did you realise he was a chance to get drafted?

Shelley Haynes: We had recruiters hanging around and player managers wanting to get Nick on board and his dad and I said, look, he hasn't been drafted yet, he doesn't need a player manager, his dad and I can look after his finances and things like that. But halfway through that season he was showing some really good form and when the player managers were knocking on our door, we knew something was coming up.

Billy: And did you hope that it was always going to be GWS because you had that orange coat in the wardrobe?

Shelley Haynes: Good question! We all grew up barracking for St Kilda, his dad and I and all of our three kids barracked for St Kilda and living in Frankston they were training at Seaford, there was a hope that he could still live at home.

Champs: He's done very well for a chap from Frankston!

Covey: In the time Nick has been up in Sydney, has he found many similarities between Frankston and Sydney? It's near the water, for example.

Shelley Haynes: Yes, there's some beaches there and he's into a surfing so wherever there's a wave he's happy.

Covey: You see the football clubs have so much control over players, I worry about Patrick Dangerfield, he goes surfing and I don't want him to hurt himself.

Shelley Haynes: They're not super keen on the boys doing anything too outrageous during the season, obviously. But in the break, that's what he does, he gets away from all of that and takes some risks.

Torch: We hear a lot about the Giants when they first started and they got all the boys to go and live at Breakfast Point, they sort of treated them like a big family. How did Nick enjoy that?

Shelley Haynes: There was the excitement of being drafted and then it was the reality that they were living in Sydney and I'm sure the boys didn't even know where Blacktown was. There's probably some similarities between Blacktown and Frankston. It was a good idea to put the boys together because can you imagine 17- to 19-year-old boys in a new big city not knowing what they were doing? I think to keep them together was a good idea. But then the boys had the choice of staying or then moving out and Nick then elected to go out and live with some of the other players.

Richo: And where do they live? What's the suburb?

Shelley Haynes: They're in Balmain, and most of the boys are around there and Rozelle. He lives with Adam Kennedy and he has lived with Adam for a number of years.

Covey: And, of course, Adam was an original too.

Shelley Haynes: Adam was an original but Adam's a bit dirty because he actually got pre-selected as a 17-year-old so he didn't actually go through the draft and get a number attached to him. So yeah, Nick is known as No. 7.

Richo: Shelley, I'm sure the family now are regular travellers up to Sydney, which you may not have been before, so have you done the Harbour Bridge climb?

Shelley Haynes: I have done that but I learned fairly quickly not to hire a car because driving in Sydney is just ridiculous.

Covey: I note you don't have the Darwin leg of your travel anymore, have you finished up your job running Netball Northern Territory?

Shelley Haynes: Yes, I finished there in August last year.

Covey: Did you lose the full support of the board?

Shelley Haynes: John and I drove back by the West Coast, we took three and a half months to come back home in our camper trailer and we were ready to come back, it ended up being four years.

Young Andy: That was very Don Pyke of you, Shelley.

Covey: Have you spoken to Nick this week? And more particularly, this morning?

Shelley Haynes: No. We decided that Sunday, Monday was the time to get the ticket situation sorted because we've got family, we've got his mates and he wants to try to accommodate that, so we got that out of the way. And then we said to him, we're going to leave you alone now for the rest of the week, you just concentrate on what you've got to do. I might text a bit later on but they're probably on a phone ban now. I gave him a text on Thursday night and that'll see him through.

Covey: Were you here last Saturday afternoon watching the game? How did you cope?

Shelley Haynes: I didn't cope! I was in the Ponsford Stand and all the play was down the far end that rugby scrum, that was so intense. I might have done a Kevin Sheedy and waved my scarf around.

Billy: You know what Nick would probably love, and this would be a top stir as well, if the Giants salute today, as he goes up to get his Premiership medallion, just wet the corner off your hanky and go up there and get a little bit of Vegemite of his face.

Shelley Haynes: Wouldn't he just love that?

Covey: In all honesty, he's a super player.

Richo: And he's had a marvellous year. Win, lose or draw, where's the function tonight?

Shelley Haynes: We're heading to Crown Palladium, we'll be down there supporting him either way.

Richo: Shelley, thank you for joining us this morning and have a great day.

MONICA MURPHY

The Western Bulldogs made history when they played their first match at Ballarat in 2017. Bulldogs star Bob Murphy was also chalking up milestones in 2017 as he passed the 300-game mark. The Ballarat match was his 310th and watching him in action was his mother Monica who followed Bob all over Australia across 18 seasons.

Richo: All roads lead to Ballarat today for an historic occasion and up there already waiting for the game is Monica Murphy. Good morning and welcome to the Coodabeens.

Monica Murphy: Good morning to you, too.

Richo: How is Ballarat, are you well rugged up?

Monica Murphy: Layer upon layer, yes, I am.

Richo: Are you at the ground already?

Monica Murphy: No, no, no, sitting down with a coffee, taking it easy.

Covey: Are there Bulldogs fans everywhere, Monica?

Monica Murphy: Absolutely. Everyone's got a Bulldogs scarf on, I think they must have sold out.

Champs: It's cold but is there any sunshine?

Monica Murphy: There was early on when we were out for a walk before and it was beautiful, a bit nippy but really beautiful.

Billy: And Mon, how does it feel to be the mother of arguably the most beloved player of the last few seasons?

Monica Murphy: I'm glad he hasn't blotted his copy book. No, it's a privilege to be his mum.

Richo: Monica, please tell us, of the 310 games, how many of you attended?

Monica Murphy: 309? No, we go to the Melbourne games, we've been to a couple in Sydney and we went over to Perth a couple of times but mostly just local games.

Covey: Well, now you can add Ballarat to the list of grounds where you saw him play.

Monica Murphy: And it might be his last.

Champs: Has Robert Murphy got a lot of siblings who have made him the class act that he is?

Monica Murphy: Yes, he has an older sister and an older brother, and they certainly moulded him and looked after him actually. I think when Robbie was two, Ben used to bowl the cricket ball full pelt as a four-year-old. He certainly was brought up with hard knocks.

Billy: Did Robert seek your counsel? Did he say, mum, I'm thinking about hanging up the boots, what do you reckon?

Monica Murphy: No. It was his own decision and he let us know, of course. We're very proud of him because we think 18 years is a pretty good innings. He just said, Look, I'm going to retire now, which we thought was great because, you know, injuries and whatever.

Richo: You're right, there comes a time. Can you go back

past that 18 years and tell us about when he was a junior player? At what stage did the family realise, gee, he might actually be able to go on with this?

Monica Murphy: There are sort of little lines in the sand, aren't there? When he first played footy, he was a basketballer and he was quite lively on the court but when he was about eight, John [Bob's dad] decided it was time he got onto the footy field, and he looked all at sea. And then suddenly in the first quarter, the ball bounced loose and I think the basketball training kicked in and he bounced with that little left hand and away he went. And John said to me, he's got it, and that was in his first little game.

Covey: Did anyone think about getting John as a recruiting officer? If he was able to spot talent after one left-handed bounce, then who knows?

Monica Murphy: Have you ever noticed that as soon as Robbie gets the ball, he does the left-hand bounce of the ball? I asked him why he does it and he said, just to get my balance.

Billy: Were you worried when he first started playing, Monica, because he was so slender, it was like he was going to snap?

Monica Murphy: At the beginning I think he used to run around and stand between Luke Darcy and Chris Grant. But when he ran onto the ground in that first game when he played against Carlton, I think everyone laughed. This little kid, skinny, just a child, but he played well.

Covey: Monica, your family is from Warragul and when Bob went up to town, how did he go having to move out of home and look after himself?

Monica Murphy: You have no idea! He had to leave school in Year 11 and we had to find a school to do his Year 12. So, he headed off to the big smoke and thank goodness Bridget and Ben were both at uni at the time and they kind of looked after him. He did Year 12, didn't have a licence, had to ride his bike.

I think Rob stayed with Ben for a little bit and then he went with Bridget who mothered him a bit.

Richo: But even though it was clear from the time Bob was eight, when he grabbed the ball for the first time, that he had it, on that first day against Carlton you couldn't have imagined that it was going to go on for 18 years.

Monica Murphy: Oh, my gosh. No. He looked like a match with all the wood scraped off. I really expected the whole crowd to stand up and cheer when he ran on, but no one did.

Champs: Well, I think that might happen today.

Monica Murphy: Oh, that'd be nice. That will make up for it.

Billy: And has he given you an indication as to what he'd like to do after footy?

Monica Murphy: In a word, no. But I'm pretty sure he will have given it plenty of thought and he'll get lots of support.

Covey: And he's probably got a bit of washing to do that he didn't bring home 18 years ago!

Richo: Monica, thank you so much for joining us this morning. I just hope you've got a nice pair of gloves or mittens.

Monica Murphy: I just bought the last pair in Ballarat, that's the truth.

Richo: Monica, have a wonderful day up there. It's a very special day in footy for a whole lot of reasons. Thank you so much for joining us.

Monica Murphy: It's a pleasure, thank you very much.

Richo: Monica Murphy there, mum of Robert.

FOOT
2021

One Or Two 'Aint Bad

SCOTT MORPHETT

Round 22, 1985 was a significant day in Coodabeens folklore because it was the day we dragged a barbecue into Victoria Park and hosted Footy Aid. If you want to know the details, we delve deeper into the story in our book The Coodabeen Champions: 40 Footy Seasons, *but for now, it was the only season that Fitzroy played home games at Victoria Park and on that day, the Lions hosted Geelong at their Lulie St temporary home. We found out 30 years later, it just happened to also be Scott Morphett's one and only game of VFL football for one kick and one goal.*

Richo: Welcome to the Coodabeens, Scott.

Scott Morphett: Thanks guys.

Covey: Scott, Covey here and Billy alongside me, we're big Cats fans. And I'd like to think I can recall every player who played for Geelong. And it might be due to the fact that on that particular day, we actually held a barbecue behind the goals at Victoria Park, and I may have been distracted from watching you get your first kick in league football.

Scott Morphett: I don't doubt that because it would have been one second of my life.

Billy: Just talk us through the goal Scott, where were you playing that day? What possie?

Scott Morphett: I waited all day and I finally got a run with about three minutes to go in the game which was wonderful. And I ran onto the ground and ran right into Superboot who picked me up and sent me on my way. And then before I knew it, Greg Williams gave me a handball and I think I just closed my eyes and kicked as hard as I could and looked up and everyone was patting me on the back.

Richo: Which end was it that you kicked it to?

Scott Morphett: It was the grandstand end.

Richo: We were behind the goals at the other end, the Yarra Falls end. I remember that because down in front of us, Gary Ablett kicked four in the first quarter.

Scott Morphett: I was sitting there watching the whole thing myself.

Torch: Who was your coach Scott, was it Tommy?

Scott Morphett: Yeah Tommy Hafey. And he was lovely and he just kind of said, well done and move on. And that was the end of the season. So it was all over.

Covey: Had you been playing in the twos all year?

Scott Morphett: Yeah, like a lot of footballers, you're in the top 22 at that stage and you think you're in but every week you're an emergency. I think I was an emergency 13 times for the year. And then I got my chance and that was it.

Billy: Where had you come from?

Scott Morphett: From Hay, NSW, a little country town.

Covey: So you've been going along in the reserves all year, you've been emergency and finally Tommy says we better have a look at this fella. Get him in for a game before next year. You've played, you've come off the bench and kicked a goal with your one and only kick.

Scott Morphett: Yep.

Covey: So then what happened?

Scott Morphett: The next week we had an elimination final in the reserves against Essendon. A guy named David Wheadon was the coach at the time and he was kind enough to put me at full back the next week on a lovely guy named Paul Salmon who was coming back from injury. And I think after six goals at quarter-time I lost count.

Covey: So you just warmed him up for his appearance in the '85 Premiership for Essendon.

Scott Morphett: Yeah I told him I was happy to help.

Covey: Did you stay on and do the next pre-season with Geelong?

Scott Morphett: Yeah, I stayed the next year but like a lot of kids, I got a stress fracture and missed most of the year and then Hafey went to Sydney and Mr Devine came in and that was the divine end of me.

Billy: Did you go back out to the bush after that?

Scott Morphett: No I sat there and felt sorry for myself for a little while and I got a call from the Eagles in South Australia to come over here and ended up having not a bad ten years over here.

Covey: Did you play in Premierships?

Scott Morphett: Two Grand Finals for one Premiership and we had a good time.

Richo: And you still live in Adelaide now?

Scott Morphett: Yeah, three kids grown up and I came for 12 months and I've been here 30 years.

Covey: So who do you follow? The Crows or the Ports?

Scott Morphett: Well not Port! I have a soft spot for the Crows but my allegiance is still Geelong.

Covey: Do you still have a few mates from your couple of years there?

Scott Morphett: Yeah, a guy who came with me over here was Gerard Toohey, he got sacked the same day I did. Which was wonderful, and we both jumped into cars and drove over to Adelaide just for a bit of fun.

Richo: And you stayed for 30 years.

Scott Morphett: Yeah, well he's now been here for 30 years as well. And he's got three kids as well. So he's just as buggered as I am!

Richo: Wonderful talking to you this morning Scott, thank you so much.

Scott Morphett: Not a problem, guys, cheers.

Richo: There you go. Another member of the Torch Club.

RON WATT

Geelong's Ron Watt was a One Game Wonder who doubled his output to become a Two Game Terrier. Ron joined Covey in the ABC commentary box at Kardinia Park one Saturday in 2009 and talked to the Coodabeens up the line. Ron was working for the Cats at the time.

Covey: Hello Ronnie, thanks for joining us to recount your two-game career at the Cats.

Ron Watt: An outstanding two games, apparently, but not outstanding enough to get another crack at it

Covey: In 1984?

Ron Watt: It's the 25th anniversary this year, Cove.

Covey: Yes, we noticed that and thought we'd better get you on. And, of course, when you made your debut it was the day before your 21st birthday.

Ron Watt: You're right.

Covey: So, did you have anything planned?

Ron Watt: Yeah, I did. I had a big party set up for the Sunday night. So, I was well prepared. I had a lot of friends who played at Geelong West in the VFA and I catered for them as well. And also an opportunity for my friends from up along the Murray River, you know, Tocumwal to come down as well.

Covey: Did making your debut put a spanner in the works for the party or just make it even better?

Ron Watt: It made it an even greater occasion. And I was pretty lucky to play in my first game at the MCG.

Covey: Wearing jumper number?

Ron Watt: 53, which was a record at the time as the highest number ever to play for Geelong.

Covey: Yeah, because Geelong always had a thing if a bloke got picked to play—and Billy you'd know this too—if you had a number higher than 40 they immediately scrambled around to find you one that was under 40 for your senior appearance.

Ron Watt: Well, I think it was a sign that I probably wasn't going to play too many games.

Billy: Next week for your second game, did they give you No. 52?

Ron Watt: No, no, I stuck with 53 because it was tradition for me. It was a jumper that passed on to Barry Stoneham who made his debut in 53 as well about five years later.

Torch: One of the reasons they might have had difficulty because I just checked the records and they were 11 debutants for Geelong in that season, and that's a lot in one year.

Ron Watt: Yeah, there were a few of us too, like Greg Williams and Gary Ablett. I think Mark Jackson made his debut for Geelong in that year.

Billy: He kicked 74 goals that year, Ron.

Ron Watt: He did. An interesting character to play with, Jacko.

Billy: You were under Tommy Hafey weren't you?

Ron Watt: I was under Tommy. He was a pretty hard taskmaster, Tommy. He would train you very, very hard but he's a terrific bloke and he always remembers you whenever he sees you. So, that was a good experience playing under Tommy.

Covey: I recall the first game of that year in '84 down here. Gary Ablett played on a wing, Jacko was full forward, Williams in the middle, Geelong kicked about 23 goals and they were on fire early in the season. I've drawn a blank from 1984—did they start turning players over because things went off the rails or something?

Ron Watt: I'm not quite sure I can't remember myself. To be honest, I think we were a bit up and down and we got a few injuries. And I managed to find my way into the team and out again pretty quickly.

Covey: So, what position did you play in your debut?

Ron Watt: Well, I think back in those days it was interchange. Yep. And I was on the bench and I think Tommy still thought it was 19th and 20th. I came on with seven minutes to go. And as soon as I ran onto the ground, my first act of play was to run up and pat Gary on the back because he'd just kicked his fourth to put us in front. I then went and picked up a young fella, Maurice Rioli, who could play a bit. We won that game and next week was at the Whitten Oval or the Western Oval as it was then. There was about three inches of rain and I played on Steve MacPherson and I think he got the three Brownlow votes. And I remember the siren broke down at half-time and they used the little league bell to stop the game and Tommy had to tap the umpire on the shoulder to tell him that half-time had occurred.

Covey: Was that the game where Gary Ablett kicked a few early and then didn't get any for the rest of the day? I reckon it was a real bog track.

Ron Watt: It was a terrible, terrible, terrible day. I think it was only about nine or ten goals scored then Jacko went off his tree and got reported by four umpires. So, it was a memorable two games for me.

Richo: So, Ron, tell us about your career up until that day in Round 11, 1984 when you came off the bench with seven minutes to go. What had you done to thrust yourself in front of the selectors down there at Geelong and get picked for your first game at almost 21?

Ron Watt: What did I do? I came down to Geelong from Tocumwal as an 18-year-old to play in the Under 19s and played there for a year. I played a few reserves games and a few reserve games the next year and they said you're not up to it and they sent me to Geelong West in the VFA for a year and then brought me back and gave me another year or so. And then next year, I think I played about five or six games then we parted company again. Actually, it's funny because David Wheadon was my reserves coach back in '85 and he always had a habit of getting Steve Hocking and I mixed up. So, between Steve and I we played 201 games. Steve played the majority of those. It's ironic though that Steve and David Wheadon and myself all work here at the Geelong footy club now We have a bit of a chuckle about it.

Covey: Twenty-five years down the track and you are very much still a part of the club and the football industry. What do you do these days?

Ron Watt: Well, I do player development now, a little bit of footy development, my game day role is managing the bench, sort of the bench coach, if you like, which I've been doing for quite a few years but most of my role is off-field development. I spend a fair bit of time with the first, second and third-year players and still play a role with all the boys across the list.

Covey: Is that their development as footballers or also developing them off the ground because you were once called the player welfare manager?

Ron Watt: Yeah, but I don't like the word welfare. So, we go with player development and it's about making the players aware or giving them the skills they need in any part of their life to actually improve and be a professional footballer. And with that comes being a good person and doing things well off-field.

Covey: Earlier today, we were talking to Peter Bosustow and he was just talking about when he was at Carlton and, you know, going to the races with Jimmy Buckley and Mark Maclure but clearly that's not part of your development role here at Geelong, Ron!

Ron Watt: Well, I have been to the races once or twice but I only stay near the boys for about an hour and then stay right out of their way but, yeah, I guess I rescue them from the races if it looks like it's becoming a common occurrence for them. It's a terrific job and a really good thing to be involved in here. You get to come and work with good young men every day and have a fair bit of fun and, yeah, it's certainly fun at the moment the way we're going.

Covey: Ron, you were saying how you came down as an 18-year-old, went through the Under 19s and then made your debut the day before your 21st birthday. Now we've got boys who have been drafted and they're playing at 18, not 21.

Ron Watt: Yeah, I was a slow developer really. I reached puberty at 18.

Billy: Ron, after your league career, did you go back out to red West?

Ron Watt: Yeah, I went back to red West and stayed with

them until they folded from the VFA. I coached the reserves team in their last year in the VFA with Gary Malarkey coaching the seniors. Then I sort of found my way into coaching more or less full-time, you know, at a local level with Geelong West-St Peters and also North Shore.

Covey: And you had great success at North Shore. How many flags?

Ron Watt: Playing coach in four flags. I'm convinced that if I hadn't had an opportunity at North Shore I wouldn't have had an opportunity to come to Geelong and have a go at the coaching back in the VFL, you know, in the early part of this century.

Covey: And it's interesting because you had four flags at North Shore and you've ended up down at Geelong and Dale Amos who is now coaching the Geelong VFL side had a similar record out at South Barwon winning three flags.

Ron Watt: Yeah, he did and he's made a terrific start to his VFL coaching career. He's very cool and explains things really well to the players and is a great development person.

Covey: So, it just goes to show, like Geelong's picked up Nigel Lappin as an assistant coach this year, a three-time Premiership player, 279 games, and at the other end of the scale for your coaching staff you go and get a local boy as well. It shows there's opportunities and you don't just have to have been at the top level.

Ron Watt: And I'd say Brendan McCartney, who is one of our other assistants, was an Ocean Grove coach, he coached them to four Premierships and has been with Geelong now for 10 years and a couple of years at Richmond before that as assistant coach.

Covey: And now, Ronnie, talking about red West. I got a call from Kevin Kirby, who's had a long association with Geelong West, to let me know that Geelong West-St. Peter's are going to wear the old Geelong West Roosters jumper for their match against Newtown on Sunday the 19th of May at the West oval.

Billy: Gee, wonderful memories of going out there every Sunday when Billy Goggin was coaching them and watching some really cracker-jack games.

Torch: Are they gonna have the bike track around the side of the oval so you can skin your knees?

Ron Watt: It's still there, they've upgraded the bike track so the bitumen sticks out a little bit further so we should see some good bloodstains there. I actually see Billy Goggin every week exercising around Eastern Beach. Still extremely fit for a man of his age.

Covey: We're hoping to get Billy on next week to talk about the Geelong West days and the fact that they're going to wear the jumper again. Kevin Kirby left a message on my phone yesterday that Billy was getting cold feet. So, if you're listening Billy, we want you on next week.

Ron Watt: Don't get Kevin Kirby on because you'll never get him off!

Covey: He rang me the other night. He said, I'll be quick. I missed a complete episode of *Four Corners*.

Champs: Ron, you said that Tommy Hafey was a very hard coach but a very good bloke. I can just see you crawling across the Geelong turf gasping your last breath saying, gee, you're a good bloke, Tommy!

Ron Watt: I remember he coached us in '83. I did part of the '83 pre-season and it was the big bushfires and we actually trained on Ash Wednesday. Yeah, we trained that evening and we ran pretty solidly for a couple of hours which is pretty dangerous really and I don't think we were allowed to have a drink either.

Covey: Even if there were water bottles Tommy would've said, don't go near them, you're not drinking any water, wouldn't he?

Ron Watt: Tommy used to always run the first four laps, there was always a four-lap warm up. Every other coach I've ever had was a two-lap warm up but Tommy was four. He'd set the pace for the first four laps and at the end of the four laps you were spent for the night.

Torch: I just had a look at the Cats' record back then and you finished just outside the five in '84 on percentage and then '85 you also finished fifth but you were a couple of games out that time. So, if Tommy hadn't have turned over so many players in '84 you might've made the finals.

Richo: If he'd given Ron a few more games, that's all they would've required.

Covey: Why were you dropped Ron? Was it ever explained to you?

Ron Watt: No, I don't know actually. That was the thing you didn't speak about in those days whereas now where everything's full-time, and you are with the players all the time, you've got no choice but to talk to them and encourage them and give them pretty good direction.

Richo: It becomes your job Ron and I'm sure when you're down on the boundary line in about an hour's time as the bench coach, you'll be tough but fair. Yeah?

Covey: Tell 'em how lucky they are to go on and off the ground unlike your first game when you had to wait until there were seven minutes to go to get a run. Just on that, what's the most rotations we have now? 80-odd?

Ron Watt: Yeah, we're usually up around 80 or so a game. We have been up to 100 at stages last year but around about 80.

Covey: How do you keep up?

Ron Watt: By the end of the game, you're actually pretty tired. You're mentally spent but it's a lot of fun. And you do get a few characters coming on and off the ground. Yeah, some of the boys are really quite humorous when they come off and some you just can't get a laugh out of, there are a couple of guys who are just deadly serious.

Richo: Well, we'll look for the body language and do a bit of lip reading. Ron, thanks so much for talking to us this arvo and have a good day there as the bench coach.

Covey: And Billy and I have always said you were hard done by, you should've played at least three games.

Ron Watt: Well, I spoke to somebody the other day who has been following Geelong since about 1976 and he's seen every game—seniors and reserves—and he couldn't remember me playing at all. So, that's probably a good sign that I'm a coach and not continuing to play.

Richo: Thanks very much, Ron. Ron Watt there two games with the Cats in Rounds 11 and 12, 1984.

CRAIG HOYER

At the end of the 1980 season, a young ruckman from Western Australia signed a Form 4 to come to Victoria and play for Hawthorn under David Parkin. When Craig Hoyer arrived in Melbourne, he was playing instead under new coach Allan Jeans and battling strong competition in the Hawks' ruck division to break into the senior side. Craig played just the one game in '81 and one in '82 before returning to Swan Districts and then on to Hobart in the Tassie league.

Richo: Welcome to the Coodabeens, Craig.

Craig Hoyer: Good morning, fellas. Thanks very much.

Richo: Tell us about your time at Hawthorn. You started off at Swan Districts?

Craig Hoyer: Yes, I started off at Swan Districts as a 17-year-old and back in those days I was signed on a Form 4 where you received a signing on fee and then signed a contract to go over and play at Hawthorn. So, I was 20 when I went over to play with Hawthorn.

Richo: Who came over and put the Form 4 under your nose?

Craig Hoyer: They had a fellow who was based in Perth, he was a scout I suppose in those days who did all the negotiation. He obviously went along to a lot of the WAFL games and was a talent scout for Hawthorn, so it was predominately done in person. I think I had one visit over and David Parkin was coaching Hawthorn so most of the negotiation was done through David. Then the year that I went over, Allan Jeans was appointed coach.

Richo: Had you known Parko when he coached in Perth?

Craig Hoyer: No, not at all. But I had a couple of meetings with David and I was really looking forward to going over and playing under him. But as it turned out, I was playing under Yabby.

Champs: They were magic times at Hawthorn in those days. Tell us about turning up for training the first night.

Craig Hoyer: As a 20-year-old it was unbelievable for me to go over there because I had very little experience in the big league. I'd played a couple of years of league footy with Swan Districts under John Todd and I went over there and I was pretty lucky to be involved in Hawthorn in that era if you have a look at some of the guys that I played reserves footy with: Gary Ayres, Peter Schwab, Chris Langford, Chris Mew, Dermott Brereton, of course, and Gary Ablett as well. And I was lucky enough to be on the end of some of the greats with Hawthorn that were coming to the end in Don Scott and Leigh Matthews, Peter Knights, Michael Tuck, those sorts of players. So, I was really lucky to be involved with the club in that period, for sure.

Billy: And that first year, 1981, at what stage of the season did you make your appearance?

Craig Hoyer: It was about halfway through the year against Essendon, it was Don Scott's 300th game, I think, out at Windy Hill.

Covey: And you got up and won it.

Craig Hoyer: Yes, we won that game, that was a great experience.

Covey: You must have been pretty stiff then to find yourself out of the side the next week.

Craig Hoyer: I think I had all of about five minutes on the ground so I obviously didn't impress enough to warrant another game.

Richo: But you did impress Hawthorn supporters that I know who were always saying to look out for Craig Hoyer and they couldn't wait for you to get a game. Who were you tussling with for a spot in the side back then? Who were the other ruckmen?

Craig Hoyer: You had Don Scott in his latter years but then they had the General, Ian Paton, who was quite a good ruckman in that period with Hawthorn and they also got a fella from Melbourne, Michael Byrne, who came across to the club as well. And big Kim Kershaw who played a lot of footy with Williamstown in the end, he was also at the club so it was tough for me. But look, some of the things that I've been able to take away from that period at Hawthorn have created an enormous amount of opportunities for me not only in footy but in life in general.

Champs: So this grounding and life education that you received at Hawthorn in the '80s, did it serve you well to go on to work for BHP Billiton?

Craig Hoyer: I'm not sure whether it stretched that far, but certainly I went back to Perth and played a couple of years back there with Swans. I then went on and played footy in Tassie for 14 years under Peter Hudson with Peter Knights and Mark Browning, those sorts of players and eventually ventured into the coaching arena and I'm still coaching one of the local sides up here.

Billy: And your second year, 1982, Craig, did you see the year out? Or did you realise halfway through the year, well, I played my game for this year and I'll look further afield or were you tapped on the shoulder?

Craig Hoyer: I guess it was a little different in those days, being a recruit from WA and things weren't going to work out as far as being a regular league player. I certainly saw the year out then I came home to WA but I guess if I was around now I would probably be shipped off to another club and, who knows, an opportunity may have created itself within another club, but it certainly didn't seem to happen as much in those days if you were an interstate player.

Torch: Craig, you mentioned that you played under Toddy over there at Swan Districts. I don't think Victorians know what high esteem John Todd is held in WA. What was he like to play under as a coach?

Craig Hoyer: Toddy's certainly a legend in WA footy. And he coached Swan Districts for a number of years and won a number of Premierships as well. I suppose he's up around the big Mal Brown status, that type of status in WA. He actually coached the Eagles, too, in the early days.

Richo: Craig, you said you're doing a bit of coaching up there locally. Locally, of course, is the Pilbara. Now where are you? Tom Price? Paraburdoo?

Craig Hoyer: I'm actually in Newman, we have a little comp here of four teams and we just have a senior side. There's about 8000 people in the town here in Newman, it's a BHP town but we are very passionate about our footy. I've coached a number of years up here and I'm coach of the side again this year. So I'm coach, my oldest son's the president and my youngest son is vice-captain.

Richo: Fantastic. And your footy season is the winter or the summer up there?

Craig Hoyer: We're winter but winter here for us is fantastic, because we don't get the rain in winter up here. All we get is sunshine, so it's the best time of the year.

Champs: Craig, are you in the executive side or do you just drive a big dump truck?

Craig Hoyer: I'm lucky enough to be in human resources, I look after all the Indigenous employment and training on site. I originally came to Newman 10 years ago to run a sports program, footy in particular, and I worked all the way through the Western Desert, right through to the Northern Territory border developing footy programs. Then I moved into the field of employment with Indigenous people and I've been with the Big Australian now for a little over five years.

Billy: Well, you said that the Newman footy clubs are a lock-out, you can only get a position of power if you're a Hoyer but you must realise, Craig, that radio's been our domain for nigh on 30 years and you've swept in and cut our lunch. You're on-air in 15 minutes halfway through our broadcast!

Craig Hoyer: Yeah, I don't know what's happened there. Obviously, we don't get to air in Victoria but I just run a local footy show for a couple of hours. Every Saturday morning we get on and have a bit of fun like you guys, I guess.

Billy: What's it called?

Craig Hoyer: *The Other Newman Footy Show*.

Richo: That is fantastic. Well, we've cut into your prep time, we've left you 16 minutes to get ready Craig. Thanks so much for talking to us today.

Craig Hoyer: Absolute pleasure, fellas. Thank you.

Richo: Craig Hoyer there on line from Newman in the Pilbara in WA about to go on air with his own radio footy show.

BILL ARMSTRONG

One of our Two Game Wonders boasted an interesting record: one game in the final round of 1958 and the other in the second round of 1959. The man in question was Carlton's Bill Armstrong who joined us 50 years later in 2009 to recall his footy journey.

Richo: Does it seem like 50 years ago, Bill?

Bill Armstrong: No, but in some way, when you watch the game today, I don't think I'd keep up with it today.

Richo: Now Bill, we've studied your statistics. There's the game you played in '58 which Carlton won and, unfortunately, it was the end of the season. The next time you played again in '59 Carlton won and you missed out the next week. In fact, that was it. Why didn't you play the next week?

Bill Armstrong: Well, I don't know. Unfortunately, he's not around to ask because I think Jack Dyer actually agreed with you and said I should have played more. But I didn't get another game. And I'm not quite sure why that was the case.

Richo: At the time, Bill, obviously, you didn't think it was gonna be your last game.

Bill Armstrong: No, I didn't. The first game I had was the last game of the season in '58, which was the year I won the best and fairest in the seconds. And I got the first game because Johnny Chick was out injured. I have some views about why I didn't… I don't think my loyalty to the club and my loyalty to football at that stage was serious enough for the club body.

Billy: You obviously didn't do a very good job of covering that up, Bill. Who was coaching at the time?

Bill Armstrong: Ken Hands was coaching in '59.

Richo: What about when you joined the Blues from Chelsea?

Bill Armstrong: I was under Jimmy Francis for most of the time there although when I first went up to Carlton it was Percy Bentley. It was the last year of Percy Bentley. I went up to Carlton in '55, '56 after Chelsea had won a Premiership. It was a fairly stormy time at Carlton, as you probably know.

Torch: And who spotted you at Chelsea and induced you to go to Carlton?

Bill Armstrong: Look, I'm not really sure who it was. I had a couple of club type guys who turned up one day at the house I was living in and told me that Carlton wanted me and they wanted to take me on the footy trip. This is 1955 just after Chelsea had won the Premiership a couple of times. I have to say honestly, I don't really remember. I know one person who was a great inspiration for me at Carlton was a guy named Jack Carney, who was ex-Geelong, wasn't he? Little Jack. And he was the coach of the seconds and he was a guy who I had a lot of respect for.

Richo: Bill, was '58 the year that John Nicholls started at Carlton?

Bill Armstrong: He started in '57. I played both my games with John. His brother Don had come down first and he played quite a few games but John I knew reasonably well. He was only a young lad, younger than I was at the time.

Richo: Could you tell then that he was gonna be something?

Bill Armstrong: Oh, yeah, he was big. He was strong. He was powerful. And he could move, he could run. I don't think I'd ever seen anyone with thighs like that when he turned up at the club.

Torch: You also played with many of the great Carlton players, blokes like Johnny James and Sergio Silvagni.

Bill Armstrong: Fantastic blokes like Brucey Comben, too. Johnny James was a great guy. Sergio Silvagni was a good friend. Johnny Benetti, of course, and I was there at the end of the career of Laurie Kerr. In fact, I always thought that Laurie hung on that bit too long and that didn't help me very much getting into the team. Johnny Chick and Graham Gilchrist were others. Graham Donaldson was a great guy, great footballer. Good, good captain.

Billy: Bill, where did your footy career go after that second and, as it turned out, last game for Carlton?

Bill Armstrong: I went to Western Australia and played a half a season with West Perth in 1960. My job took me to Western Australia. So I transferred over and played that year, West Perth were Premiers that year. I played half the season then broke my leg in the middle of the season. So that finished me there. Then I went back to Chelsea where I'd come from. And I played from '61 till '63 and Chelsea were Premiers in '62 and '63. Then I went to East Burwood because I moved to East Burwood to live and I played my last season '64 with East Burwood and again they were Premiers. I'm one of those lucky footballers who actually played in four Grand Finals and won them all.

Richo: And there's plenty who've played in none and won none. The move to Western Australia was a big enough thing to do way back then. But your work since for Australian Volunteers International has taken you even further west over to South Africa and, Bill, you've been involved with introducing Australian footy to South Africa.

Bill Armstrong: Yes, Australian Volunteers International has worked with the AFL and Brian Dixon and others to provide people to go over there as coaches for young kids. But, of course, the history of Australian rules football in South Africa goes back to the gold rush days when there were thousands of people playing Australian rules football in South Africa, I believe. It was imported with the gold rush but, yes, Australian Volunteers International provided a number of people who have gone there as junior coaches.

Torch: Are you still following Carlton?

Bill Armstrong: Oh, yeah, I'm still a Blue boy. I'm a member. I don't get to the games as often as I'd like. But now with my grandchildren growing up and being reasonably successful in getting most of them to follow Carlton, I'm beginning to go to see them play.

Richo: Long may you enjoy it and thanks for joining us this morning, Bill.

Bill Armstrong: Thanks very much for that.

Playin' For The Saints

PAT MURPHY

The year 1966 was an auspicious one for St Kilda. Many pundits had regarded the Saints as the best team in the caper in '65 but they fell short against Essendon on the last day in September. Breaking into the star-studded line-up was a big challenge but Pat Murphy managed to do so albeit for one game only. And that just happened to be against Collingwood at Victoria Park. Pat became a football journeyman playing in South Australia, the Northern Territory and Western Australia. We caught up with him in Adelaide.

Richo: Morning, Pat.

Pat Murphy: Morning boys, how are you?

Covey: Yeah, terrific, what about yourself?

Pat Murphy: Yeah, good. I'm over in sunny Adelaide at the moment. It's great.

Covey: Have you gotten over the fact you just played the one game all those years ago yet?

Pat Murphy: Well, actually, I don't know if I really qualify because I didn't play the full game.

Covey: Tell us what happened.

Pat Murphy: Well, I was 19 at the time, and from the age of 13 I wore spectacles and was very short-sighted and the club was good enough to buy me some contact lenses in about '65, I think. I was using those on the fateful day. I got to the rooms, got changed and put them in and was interviewed by Geoff Leek the ex-Essendon champion and commentator. Then I looked away and thought I can only see out of one eye. One had flicked out in the change rooms and we couldn't find it.

Torch: Now Patty, it's Torchy here.

Pat Murphy: G'day Torch, how are you?

Torch: Good mate. Now I was told by a mutual friend of ours that you had Darrel Baldock, Ian Stewart and Carl Ditterich on their hands and knees looking for your contact lens.

Pat Murphy: Yeah, and I think Yabby might have been amongst it as well! All to no avail. So Yabby asked me, do you still want to play? And, so, I took out the other one and said, yeah, as you would. The problem was that I couldn't decipher colours or read the scoreboard or whatever. And it made it a bit difficult in your first game.

Richo: And it wasn't your fault alone, though, that St Kilda lost the game by 12 goals.

Pat Murphy: I remember that part vividly because, correct me if I'm wrong, but I'm pretty sure it's the week after the interstate game. And Baldock and Stewart really both probably shouldn't have played. They were injured, I think. And they didn't get into it. In fact, again, I hope I remember this correctly but we were going so bad that day that I think Daryl Griffiths got the ball at one stage and burst through the middle, bounced once and kicked the ball 60 metres the wrong way.

Torch: Now, even though you couldn't see at Victoria Park, I'm sure you could hear. Can you remember any of the little comments that were coming across the boundary line at you?

I THINK
BIG CARL MIGHT
BE STANDING ON
MY CONTACT LENS!
SORRY LAD,
BUT THERE'S NO WAY
I'M ASKING HIM
TO MOVE...

Pat Murphy: Yeah, I remember a little comment as we ran out of the race. Well, it wasn't really a comment but we were spat on by a couple of Collingwood supporters. That was a good introduction. It was all a bit surreal because it was sort of, you know, I couldn't see a lot and the roar of the crowd sort of goes from one side of the ground to the other. You don't hear a lot of individual voices out there.

Billy: Pat, did the Collingwood players twig that you couldn't see?

Pat Murphy: I don't think it mattered but I don't really know.

Billy: They didn't say hey, look, No. 49 is blind as a bat, play through him!

Richo: Pat, there you are, it's Round 10 of an 18-game season. St Kilda, even though they've lost that day at Victoria Park are travelling very, very well in what ended up being a Premiership year. At the time, you wouldn't have thought it was going to be your last game.

Pat Murphy: No, well, I guess I was 19, pretty young and I thought I might get another chance but fate wouldn't have it that way. But I really felt that probably five years later, I was a far better player than I was as a 19-year-old then.

Richo: Five years later, where were you, Pat?

Pat Murphy: I actually went from St Kilda in '67 and I was a playing coach in Gippsland for three years. And then I came over here to South Australia and played for South Adelaide for a year and the next couple of years I went to Darwin. I probably played my best three years of footy in that time, I guess. I was in my mid-20s and I suppose most players mature and play their best footy around about then, don't they?

Billy: And when you were playing that best football, was it in contact lenses? Or did you go the Geoff Blethyn and tape the specs to your head, Pat?

Pat Murphy: You wouldn't believe this but, coincidentally, the first game at St Mary's in Darwin I lost a contact lens while I was playing.

Torch: Having played a lot of junior football with you, I do know how good you were when you were a young player, so I think you're probably downgrading your ability. Now, I believe that you spent a lot of time working up there in the Northern Territory after you finished with St Mary's. What sort of jobs were you doing?

Pat Murphy: Oh, I was in the public service. And when I left Adelaide, it was really to play the off-season because, of course, that's played in the wet season. I intended to go back to Adelaide but got a job in the public service and was able to travel and, subsequently, in '74 I played in a combined Darwin side that played South Fremantle. So, I actually ended up going down to Perth and playing a season with South Fremantle in '74, and I was 28 then. So the job enabled me to sort of travel a fair bit and so on which was really good.

Richo: Going back to that side, you ran out at Victoria Park in 1966. You just casually tossed off some names like Daryl Griffiths. It was an unbelievably exciting footy team St Kilda in '66, wasn't it?

Pat Murphy: It certainly was. Just to be able to train alongside guys like Darrel and Ian, you know, they were absolutely fantastic. I remember doing a little bit of pre-season work with Ian Stewart and running the Caulfield race track. We used to do it in the mornings on a couple of days a week or something and he was an absolute champion. And oh so many of them. Cowboy Neale was fantastic, in fact, Yabby's perfect footballer would be Cowboy. You know, that's the style of guy he liked and as a test on the Thursday before a game, I can remember playing some man-on-man against Cowboy. That was a hell of a test, lucky Cowboy was such a nice guy because I probably wouldn't have made my debut if he got serious!

Covey: Because you were 169cm and 70kg when you made your debut. That means you're spotting Cowboy a fair bit of height and weight, I'd suggest.

Pat Murphy: Yeah, I think I came up to about his nipple! But a hell of a nice guy, Cowboy.

Covey: Do you keep an eye on them today, Pat?

Pat Murphy: Actually, I went down and watched the Hawks-Saints game in Launceston and I didn't realise they were having their show on Friday night and I sort of found out about it on the late Saturday or Sunday and I would have loved to have caught up with them, of course. It would have been good to see them again. I played a lot of school football with Breeny, he was a De La Salle boy.

Torch: And Teddy Schwarzman, was he around?

Pat Murphy: Actually, Ted and I were plucked out of schoolboy footy and played our first reserves game at the end of 1963 to sort of get us down to the club.

Richo: A lot of romantics in football have really got their fingers crossed for a St Kilda-Collingwood Grand Final this year. Will you come across from Adelaide if that happens?

Pat Murphy: Oh, yes, we've already got tickets and flights booked, we did that early in the season. We do it every year.

Richo: And you reckon the Saints can do it?

Pat Murphy: I think so. Yeah, I really do, I think last week was a bit of a glitch. I think he might be working them fairly hard at this point and back off in a week or two.

Richo: Win, lose or draw, Pat, make sure you go down to the rooms afterwards. You never know, you might find that contact lens. Pat Murphy there, he played one game for the Saints against Collingwood in 1966.

BILL CANNON

Bill Cannon is a One Game Wonder thanks to his lone appearance for St Kilda in Round 18 in 1975 when the Saints played host to Geelong at VFL Park, Waverley. Bill's name was familiar with the fans due to his journalistic pedigree, his uncle Jack being a prominent media identity.

Richo: Good morning to the man in the No. 24 jumper, Bill Cannon.

Bill Cannon: Morning boys.

Covey: How are you, Billy? Who would have thought that you'd have to wait 34 years to be interviewed?

Bill Cannon: And you got the number wrong, boys. It was 47. And Grant Thomas had 48, so I obviously had him covered.

Richo: Well, we will alert the authorities because you're down in the book as wearing 24.

Covey: Can you just talk us through the build-up to your selection for your debut, Bill?

Bill Cannon: Well, probably I had no idea I was going to be selected and I was having treatment for a crook knee and one of the physios suggested I should go out and train because there were a few older blokes struggling to come up. So, I went out and we were doing match practice and I was put on Allan Davis, who subsequently made way for me in the team and he obviously had wind of what was going to happen and every time the ball came our way he did his best to punch me in the back of the head, drive my head into the ground, that sort of stuff. But I survived that and I only found out on the Thursday night when Scot Palmer from *The Sun* rang me up about 10.30pm just to let me know that I'd been picked.

Richo: But you were already working at *The Herald* at the time weren't you, Bill?

Bill Cannon: Yeah, I was a cadet journo at *The Herald* at that stage.

Covey: Why didn't you break your own story?

Bill Cannon: Well, it would've been difficult because *The Herald* was an afternoon paper and I got picked on the Thursday night, Covey!

Covey: You could've tipped it for the early edition saying 'It will be interesting to watch St Kilda training tonight to see whether young Bill Cannon is selected'.

Bill Cannon: Yeah, that's right but Scotty got the scoop.

Richo: Of course, not just St Kilda fans but everybody studying the teams in the paper that Friday morning recognised the name because they were all familiar with the name Bill Cannon already.

Bill Cannon: Yeah, but I'm not too sure I'd had too many bylines at that stage. I think I was just doing the shipping round and getting the pizzas for the chief of staff at lunchtime. That was about the limit of my exposure in the papers at that stage.

Billy: You'd probably learnt to spell Oriana and Castel Felice.

Bill Cannon: I tell you what was hard, doing the tides. For Port Phillip and Western Port, you had to add an hour 23 to Western Port except when it went into the next day. I kept doing the tides and the copy taker who was an old bloke named Allan Baines said, 'Listen, son, you better get this right. Because if the fishermen went out at the time you suggested it was going to be high tide, they're never going to get back in let alone catch any fish'. So, I just used to leave Western Port blank and let him fill in.

Richo: Bill, tell us about your junior footy career and what landed you at the Saints?

Bill Cannon: Well, basically, I was playing for Brighton Grammar and we played against Scotch College at Scotch and a guy, I think his name was Ken Walker, just approached me after the game. It was the first game of the year in what would have been '73 and invited me to come down to St Kilda and train a couple of times. And then I got the job at *The Herald* and I presumed you couldn't play sport on Saturdays because you had to work. So, I didn't play any footy in '74. We played a few social games and a few of the guys mentioned that they saw I knew what I was doing. So, I told them I'd trained with St Kilda, etc. and the chief of staff said, probably in early '75, you'd better go and have a crack at playing footy. I did that and got that game, pretty luckily probably because, as I said, there was a few injuries but I played that game in Round 18, beat Geelong by four points and got the flick the next week when we played Footscray at Footscray and George Young played his first game at full forward ever. He kicked nine goals on Gary Merrington, and every goal he kicked was another nail in the coffin. So, I never graced the senior team again. And George Young became one of the great full forwards at St Kilda.

Richo: So how long after that did you continue on at the Saints?

Bill Cannon: Well, I played right through to the end of '75 in the seconds. Doug Booth and I were picked out by Allan Jeans to do a huge pre-season, just the two of us and Jeansy. We're wrestling and doing 400s and all this sort of stuff. And in a practice match at the start of '76 we're playing Carlton, I'm pretty sure it was a seconds practice match, and Vin Waite was playing for Carlton. He was a huge bloke and I thought I'd make a hero of myself at about 12 stone and I tried to run through him. It didn't work and I ended up having a knee reconstruction from the collision and basically that finished me. I had a go late in '76 and in '77 played a few more reserves games and Mike Patterson came to the club at the start of '78 and said I think you've had your time son. I went down to Frankston in the Mornington Peninsula league with Travis Payse who was the president and Paddy Flaherty coached them and I finished playing there. We got beaten in a Preliminary Final by Gerard Healy's Edithvale-Aspendale and then I went overseas for a couple of years trying to make a name as a journo.

Covey: And how did that go?

Bill Cannon: That went pretty well! I did the British Open the year that Seve Ballesteros won it out of the car park and the final at Wimbledon where Bjorn Borg beat Roscoe Tanner in five sets.

Torch: And how did Boothy go, did he hang around for a bit longer than you did?

Bill Cannon: Yeah, I've got a good story about Boothy. We were playing an intra-club match and Boothy came around to my place because he lived around the corner in Brighton. We go into the game and he picked out one bloke and he said I'm going to knock this bloke out because I don't like him. So, we get the jumpers handed out and he got a red jumper and I got a blue jumper and the bloke he wanted to knock out got a red jumper so he's on Boothy's team. Obviously it was going to be hard for Boothy to knock this bloke out. So, Boothy and I line up on each other and I was going for the ball and he just belted me right behind the ear. And I said what's all that about and he said well mate, if I can't get the other bloke I might as well give you a belt! We all remember the story of Boothy kicking the dog at Waverley. He's now a professor at a New Zealand university.

Covey: Did you play at full forward in your one senior game?

Bill Cannon: Yes, I did, I played full forward against John Scarlett. I read the *Football Life* magazine in the week leading up to the game and there was a story about the toughest six defenders in the VFL and he was about number four. I walked down to full football with Cowboy Neale and he introduced me to Scarlett: 'Gunner, this is a young kid from Brighton Grammar playing his first game.'

Covey: You were the Jack Watts!

Bill Cannon: I was the Jack Watts. Though Wattsy's played two now so he's got me covered. And he's kicked two goals so he's two in front of me. Anyway, Scarlett was having a bit of a chat and talking about the camber of the ground at Waverley and, you know, it's a bit wide on the flanks and you've got to be careful… he's not a bad bloke. And just as Kevin Smith bounces the ball, he punched me right in the gob. Thankfully he strained a hamstring halfway through the first quarter and I was lucky enough to have Phil Baker come down to full back so for the next hour and a half all he did was jump on my head and take speccies.

Torch: How were you off for size? Because Johnny Scarlett was a fair size of a bloke.

Bill Cannon: I tell you, if you think he was a fair size, 'Snake' Baker had arms as big as my legs. He was scary and I don't know whether you remember but a few years later he was playing at North and he kicked about five in the Grand Final on Kel Moore and made Kel Moore look like an average player.

Richo: And, of course, everyone remembers that photograph of Ron Barassi's whiteboard before the game with 'long bombs to Snake on it'. But, Bill, there's one part of that story that I'm finding difficult to understand. You walk down to full forward. Cowboy Neale's introduced you to Gunner Scarlett. Wasn't Cowboy gonna stand next to Gunner Scarlett himself?

Bill Cannon: Actually, I'll tell you what did happen later in the game. I was going for the ball near the boundary line and Sam Newman tried to put me over the fence. And he was halfway there to doing it when Cowboy came in and basically nearly threw Sam over the fence. It was pretty handy to have Cowboy because at that stage he would have been about eighteen and a half stone and Gunner looked like a stick insect compared to him and probably Snake did, too, although Snake had the biggest biceps I've ever seen.

Covey: Now fast forward to tomorrow. You're still obviously a very strong Saints man, Billy. And who would have thought that game all those years ago would set the foundation for this crackerjack game tomorrow.

Bill Cannon: Exactly, but I'm not able to go because I've got Fox Sports commitments. So what I generally do is watch as much as I can at home but I wouldn't mind going. I think it'll be a cracker of a game.

Covey: And apart from watching them do you get down to the club at or catch up with any of the blokes you played with?

Bill Cannon: Not much. The past players have an occasional function here and there and I catch up with a few of the boys, Robert Muir and a few of those blokes.

Covey: Would it be fair to say that the Saints players don't really need to catch up and have reunions because they did all their work when they were actually playing.

Bill Cannon: You probably remember the times we had down at that Moorabbin social club.

Covey: The Saints disco!

Bill Cannon: I don't know where they go now but we had a fair bit of fun at that Saints disco!

Covey: By the way, did you like playing at Waverley?

Bill Cannon: Yeah, it wasn't bad. I mean, it was a ground that you actually had to play on a bit, I would imagine, because it was a hell of a lot wider and there was a camber. The day I played I think Rex Hunt was playing up the other end at centre half-forward for Geelong and from where I was standing at full forward you only saw him from his waist up. It was a good ground, a big ground, and I would have liked to have played on it a bit more because there's a lot of space to keep out of the way.

Richo: Well, if they still had Waverley going, they could have squeezed a lot more people into the game tomorrow. Billy, all the very best.

Bill Cannon: Thank you very much, boys.

Richo: Bill Cannon, one game for St Kilda in 1975.

CHRIS STONE

The so-called 'exclusive' club of players who kicked a goal with their first kick in league football is overflowing these days. The real exclusivity rests with those who have kicked two *goals with their first* two *kicks. Ex-St Kilda player Chris Stone joined that elite group back in 1978. We caught up with him in Belgium, the time difference meaning it was well after midnight when he joined us for a chat.*

Richo: Hello Chris, thanks for getting up so early in the morning to talk to us.

Chris Stone: I didn't get up. I went out to a restaurant and I got back about half an hour ago. So, I didn't have to get up at all. I stayed up.

Richo: Chris, you've been living in Belgium for 20 years. We're a bit disappointed that you haven't picked up a Belgian accent.

Chris Stone: I can speak French if you like but when I try and do that my kids just laugh at me.

Billy: Can you cast your mind back to 1978?

Chris Stone: It was a Queen's Birthday weekend out at Waverley against Collingwood. I think I was 19th or 20th man and we were getting beaten quite easily and I came on halfway through the last quarter and I think I was playing on Max Richardson. I took a mark and got a goal and then the ball came down again, George Young handballed it to me and I scored a second goal.

Billy: And you started to think how easy is this caper?

Chris Stone: I thought, well, this is alright. In front of 70-75,000 people for my first game.

Champs: What happened the next week?

Chris Stone: Next week was Carlton at Princes Park. I got in the 18 that game and lined up on the half-forward flank and was picked up by a certain Alex Jesaulenko.

Billy: Kept you quiet did he, Chris?

Chris Stone: Pretty much—I ended up in hospital before half-time.

Champs: What happened?

Chris Stone: Graeme Bond had the ball and I was shepherding him and Jezza pushed me into the line of the ball and so the ball hit me in the eye and I got carried off and rushed to hospital with a detached retina and a haemorrhage behind the eye and had to spend two weeks flat on my back in hospital with two eye patches on.

Richo: But that didn't stop your career because you played wearing special glasses, didn't you?

Chris Stone: Yes, I did. So that was the end of the '78 season and I was playing district cricket for St Kilda in the off season. In the second last game, which would have been about February, I was fielding at silly point before the days of helmets and I got a ball directly into the same eye so I ended up in the same hospital with the same nurses and the same doctors for another two or three weeks with patches on.

Covey: 1980 was your best year, you played 15 games before Jezza took over as coach. Did he remember actually pushing you into the line of that ball?

Chris Stone: I did remind him, but I didn't get many games after that!

Richo: So, after those two injuries you then went back to football and played wearing specialised eyewear.

Chris Stone: Yeah, there was a doctor who thought that it'd be a good idea if I wore squash goggles. And it was successful in that I didn't get another knock in the eye but I did get a lot of nicknames.

Billy: And Chris, did you find it hard to follow the path between district cricket and VFL football?

Chris Stone: Yeah, it was tough. You couldn't do both properly so I favoured more the football side of it.

Billy: You must have done okay, you managed to play cricket for St Kilda for 10 years.

Chris Stone: St Kilda and South Melbourne and then when I went up to Sydney and played cricket for Manly. But football was my first love.

Richo: Now that Jezza era, when he was coaching, it was incredibly exciting at the start not just for St Kilda supporters but for everybody.

Chris Stone: It was when he replaced Mike Patterson. Foxy [president Lindsay Fox] came in after we didn't start the season terribly well and after the second or third game, he changed Mike Patterson for Alex Jesaulenko. The first few games under Jezza we were playing out of our skin, we played very well. And then it all fell away, I think there were too many younger players who didn't have enough experience.

Richo: I remember there was the famous incident where a couple of St Kilda players ran into each other in front of the members and that sort of finished it for Lindsay.

Chris Stone: Yeah, I think I was one of them!

Billy: You're kidding.

Chris Stone: No, and I've kept that quiet, I've never told anyone.

Covey: That could be one of the great trivia questions because everyone's heard that story. Now everyone knows one of them was Chris Stone.

Richo: We know about the squash goggles and the two goals from your first two kicks, but this is the real story.

Billy: Who was the other play that ran into you?

Chris Stone: That's it! He ran into me.

Richo: It changed the whole history of the club.

Chris Stone: And I can't remember who it was.

Covey: We'll find out through Russell Holmesby. It was a wonderful era. Did you ever get yourself up to the Saints disco after a game, Chris?

Chris Stone: That was pretty much our objective at the end of each game, we just wanted to get the footy over and get up to the disco!

Billy: And Chris, what took you to Belgium?

Chris Stone: I'm in advertising. So when I left Australia, I was employed by a French advertising group and worked in the UK, in Europe and then in France. And then I came to Belgium for three years and I haven't found my way out yet.

Billy: I believe you've got an interest in Belgian federal politics as well.

Chris Stone: Yeah. Well, I don't but my wife does. She's a federal MP. Her name is Sophie Wilmes.

Richo: So, Denmark's got Princess Mary and Belgium's got you.

Chris Stone: And Australia's finance minister is a guy named Mathias Cormann who is Belgian.

Richo: Yeah, and he's got a much more fetching accent than you, Chris.

Billy: Although funnily enough after so long in Belgium, you have a distinct accent.

Chris Stone: In which way?

Billy: Well, it's not quite the full Mathias, but there is certainly an inflection there. I don't know whether your Australian family tell you that.

Chris Stone: They do but after a few days and a few beers with friends that sort of switches back into the standard approach. No, it's true, people do say I've got a bit of an English accent.

Champs: Do you still follow the Saints?

Chris Stone: I do. I'm still in touch with a few of the boys from time to time. Mark Kellett, Kenny Sheldon, Rod Butterss. Barry Breen's coming over and playing golf in Turkey. So, I'm going to go down and play some golf with him in a few months.

Richo: I know it's nearly 3am there and you'll have to be getting up in about two or three hours' time to watch the Saints when the game comes on live. It's been wonderful talking with you Chris, thank you so much.

Chris Stone: Thanks for the call guys.

The Kids Are Alright

DENIS HUGHSON

One game, one kick, one goal, one quarter, career over with a knee injury. Denis Hughson is the ultimate 'what if' in league football. The son of a Fitzroy legend, 1944 Premiership captain Fred, he travelled to Melbourne from Warrnambool to play in the ones only to do a knee early in the second quarter against St Kilda at Moorabbin. Denis joined us in 2015 to talk us through the goal he kicked with his first, and only, kick in league footy.

Richo: Welcome to the Coodabeens, Denis.

Denis Hughson: Thank you very much.

Richo: Tell us about what happened before you took that kick. What was your background? Who had you played for and how did you get to Fitzroy?

Denis Hughson: I played for South Warrnambool in the Hampden league.

Champs: The Roosters?

Denis Hughson: That's right. And in 1964 we won the Grand Final and the following year Terry Board went to Carlton and Kevin Neale went to St Kilda and Fitzroy weren't travelling very well at the time and probably thought to themselves, if they went down and got a game, I might be good enough to have a try.

Richo: So, do you remember who rang you up from Fitzroy?

Denis Hughson: Harry Meese was the fella. He came down to see me and asked if I would be interested in having a game and I jumped at the chance.

Torch: Denis, Hughson is a very famous name at Fitzroy. Their last Premiership team in 1944 was captained by a fella named Fred Hughson. Any relation?

Denis Hughson: Father.

Torch: Were there father and son picks in those days?

Denis Hughson: No, but they rang dad up first to see if I'd be interested in going down to Melbourne.

Covey: So, you got the double Denis. You're a father-son player at the same club and you kick a goal with your first kick. How old were you when you came up to Fitzroy?

Denis Hughson: I was 20.

Richo: And where did Fitzroy put you up?

Denis Hughson: They didn't put me up at all! I travelled down by train to Melbourne on the Friday and stayed at my aunty's place in Brunswick. And then I travelled by train down to Moorabbin on Saturday morning.

Billy: And the game was down at Moorabbin. That would have been St Kilda's first year at Moorabbin. Am I correct?

Denis Hughson: Yes, that's right.

Champs: So, you had to get yourself to the ground? No one was picking you up?

Denis Hughson: No, I got the train down to Moorabbin and I think I got a taxi from the train station to the footy ground.

Richo: Had you trained with Fitzroy?

Denis Hughson: Earlier in the year, I'd played in their practice games.

Richo: Who was coaching?

Denis Hughson: Billy Stephen. Kevin Murray at the time was over in Perth.

Covey: Tell us about the game, Denis.

Denis Hughson: Well, I can't remember much about it. I only played a quarter. I was picked as a rover. And I was sitting in the forward pocket. The ball hadn't come down all day and I'm waiting and waiting and waiting. And finally the ball came down and I went to take an easy mark and I spilled it. Anyway, I got the ball back and kicked a goal. And then I was roving with Johnny Newnham and he said to me, 'Do you want to start off roving in the second quarter?' and I said 'Yeah I'll start that off'. And I think the first time I went for the ball someone fell across my leg and that was it, that was the finish.

Richo: And you never played again.

Denis Hughson: No, I never played down there, I came back and played at South Warrnambool.

Torch: And how long were you out with that knee injury before you could play again?

Denis Hughson: I missed probably a couple of months, then I came back and tried to play and it was no good. And then I came back down to Melbourne and had an operation. And then after that I came back and finished my career with South.

Billy: Was it a cartilage you had done Denis?

Denis Hughson: Yeah. And in those days when you had a cartilage done it was pretty desperate.

Covey: And look at how it's all changed now, they would have fixed you up straight away.

Denis Hughson: In those days people said keep off your leg for a couple of weeks, these days straight away you're up and about, aren't you?

Richo: So, one game, one goal.

Denis Hughson: One kick, one quarter ...

Richo: And it was at Moorabbin, it's just a shame it didn't all happen at Brunswick Street.

Denis Hughson: That's right. But we played all the practice games at Brunswick Street.

Champs: South Warrnambool Roosters have a very strong history in the Hampden league. Did you win a few flags there?

Denis Hughson: Yeah, a lot of flags.

Billy: You grew up in in a Fitzroy family so has that continued, did you follow the Lions up to Brisbane?

Denis Hughson: I don't see that many games but I probably see a couple of games a year. My two brothers played for Fitzroy as well, Gary played Under 19s and my other brother Fred played in the reserves.

Richo: Denis, it's been tremendous talking to you this morning. And your story highlights just how much of what goes on in footy can just be the smallest thing that can go one way or another. You kick a goal with your first kick thinking how good is this, and a few minutes later your career is effectively ended by an on-field accident. It's a cruel game.

Denis Hughson: But then again, I was lucky enough to get there.

Richo: You did it. Denis, thanks again.

Denis Hughson: Thank you.

Richo: Denis Hughson, whose father also played for Fitzroy.

Torch: Premiership captain.

Richo: Kicked a goal with his first kick and it was the only game he played.

Champs: So, when you asked him was he related to Fred and he said 'Father', you could say they were genuinely related!

GRANT OPPY

The son of Tigers legend Max, Grant Oppy made his debut for Richmond in 1970 after back-to-back Premierships with the Under 19s. A combination of injuries and a very strong senior line-up curtailed his career at that single game in the ones, but had Grant hit Royce Hart up on the lead rather than take a shot at goal for himself, could things have been different?

Richo: Joining us now on the Coodabeen Champions is Grant Oppy. Welcome and good morning, Grant.

Grant Oppy: Good morning.

Richo: Grant you went through a time when the Richmond Under 19s were just about unbeatable.

Grant Oppy: We were. In '68 and '69, I think we only lost three games.

Billy: Was that under Slug Jordon, Grant?

Grant Oppy: Yeah, under Slug. I can remember the last game of the year in '69, we got beaten by Footscray out at the Western oval. And because we were that far in front on the ladder, they'd organised a trip to South Australia for us in between that game and the second semi-final. And Slug was so bloody upset that he cancelled our trip away.

Covey: Well, that is a knee-jerk reaction.

Torch: He obviously didn't subscribe to the idea that you needed to lose one before the finals.

Grant Oppy: No I don't think he did. I also think the boys were just trying not to get injured so that we could all front up for the second semi, but we didn't expect that result.

Billy: What was it about Slug that young men could relate to so well?

Grant Oppy: I can quite vividly remember him coming out with Graeme Richmond to our house to talk to me about coming down from school to play in the Under 19s. And you know, Graeme brought my mother a box of chocolates and kept telling us what a wonderful son I was, etc. And I can remember the first game I played, I went down to South Melbourne and at half-time Slug said you can play in the centre. I think we were about 12 or 14 goals in front at half time and I think from memory I'd picked up a few touches and I thought I'd done alright. And he lined us all up after the game and went through everybody player by player and he got to me and he said as for you young Oppy, if you don't begin to chase, etc, you'll be back playing paddock football at your expletive, expletive school. And I can remember from then on for the rest of the time I spent in the Under 19s, if I had to chase, I'd chase.

Richo: And then by 1970, you're breaking into what was then a reigning Premiership side, so had you been elevated to the senior list by that stage?

Grant Oppy: I was elevated to the senior list at the beginning of the year and in those days, the ones trained by themselves on Thursday night and the magoos would be sent down to the dark end of Punt Road oval. And I think Mr. Cooke, who was chairman of selectors at that stage, he said on Tuesday night you'll be training with the senior team.

Champs: You must have gone alright in the twos in Round 8 then.

Grant Oppy: Yeah, I must have gone all right and probably got a few touches.

Covey: You were the son of a legend in Max, of course, a Richmond life member and member of the Hall of Fame and everything, but I can't quite recall the newspaper and media coverage at a time. Was there a build-up because you were the son of Max?

Grant Oppy: I think there was a photo in the paper but that wasn't such a big thing back then. They were pretty good about that at Richmond, they knew my dad was a great player at the club but for most of the time, the boys that I played with were pretty good about accepting me.

Torch: Well, obviously, Max's influence didn't account for much because your only got one game!

Grant Oppy: That's right, yeah.

Richo: Tell us about that one Grant.

Grant Oppy: I sat on the bench with Ray Ball and it was a pretty close game. I think Cuddles went on before me and then in the last quarter Graeme Richmond was sitting on the bench with Tommy and he said take your dressing gown off and on I went. I played on Denis Pagan and got a couple of kicks. I can remember taking a mark in the forward line. Royce led out and I didn't pass to him. I took a shot at goal instead and the ball passed over the top of the goal post for a point. That wasn't a good career move was it? I often think if I'd passed to Royce, what my career could have been!

Billy: Tommy said put your dressin' gown back on!

Champs: Now Grant, obviously at the time it was your first game, on the MCG, you didn't think it was going to be your last game?

Grant Oppy: No, I didn't, but I had a few injury problems after that and eventually I went to Port Melbourne.

Torch: Who was involved in getting you down to Port?

Grant Oppy: I can't quite remember, I think it was Alan Schwab. I played as an amateur down at Richmond. And I can remember when I got my final pay cheque, I got $27 for that senior game and we used to get $12 I think in the Under 19s.

Richo: Oh, so you played as an amateur, but they kept it all in trust for you.

Grant Oppy: Yes. I can remember when I eventually went down to Port Melbourne, Alan called me into the office and gave me a check for four years, two in the Under 19s and a couple of years in senior football, and I think it was a grand total of about 800 bucks, which was a lot of money in those days.

Richo: Mike Perry, Premiership centre half-back for Richmond, said recently that your AFL career can be very short but you're a past player forever.

Grant Oppy: Exactly right. And when my dad passed away in December the club were absolutely fantastic. Especially Mike, he was terrific, and the past players at Richmond are great about looking after people that have played 300 games or people who have played one.

Covey: And it must be something about the Oppy name and the Richmond profile because when young Andy our producer said he'd lined you up to be our One Game Wonder today I said, 'Grant Oppy? He played more than one game!' Because it's in my memory bank as if you'd played a lot more footy than that. Maybe it was just watching the VFA on a Sunday afternoon.

Grant Oppy: Possibly. As they say, my father and I played a couple of hundred games between us. Which is always a nice label. People often ask me, 'Did you play football?' And I say, 'Yeah', and they say, 'Oh, I can't remember you, I remember your dad though'.

Torch: When the name Max Oppy was mentioned, people shivered a bit but I don't know if they did the same when they mentioned your name Grant?

Grant Oppy: Well, probably not because I had a fairly short career but I did try to play the game the same way.

Billy: How long were you down at Port, Grant?

Grant Oppy: A couple of seasons. And then I went down and coached Sorrento. I ran into a few knee problems at Port Melbourne.

Billy: Yeah, other people's knees!

Grant Oppy: Well I did play on the half-back line with Georgie Allen and Bobby Profitt.

Covey: You played in an era when they had some great players, Grant

Grant Oppy: Great players and pretty hard too. Bobby Mallett at full back and Fred Cook up forward. Buster Harland and Billy Swan too.

Richo: It certainly was a golden era. Grant, thank you so much for joining us, and sharing all those memories of 1970 and your one game.

Grant Oppy: Thanks very much.

STEPHEN BICKFORD

Stephen Bickford was the son of a Demons' Premiership player when he was recruited via the father/son rule in the late '70s. His dad George played in the 1948 Premiership side among his 126 games but Stephen had a harder time of it, playing 15 senior games across two seasons in 1980 and '81. Stephen joined us in 2015 in our segment, The Kids Are Alright.

Richo: Stephen Bickford, welcome to the Coodabeens.

Stephen Bickford: Thanks, gentlemen.

Covey: Hello, Bicky.

Stephen Bickford: Hello Ian, I've been listening to you.

Covey: I told you I'd get you on here one day. Tell us about your dad George and his career.

Stephen Bickford: George was a great sportsman. George's father also played in the VFL, he played a couple of games for Essendon at the turn of the century. Footy was in our family, Dad's uncle Rod McGregor was in the Team of the Century for Carlton and George went straight from Wesley and started in '44, was vice-captain and played in the '48 Premiership which was the drawn Grand Final and replay, and then he retired at 25 when he got married.

Champs: Did he give up footy completely?

Stephen Bickford: He did. He went and wrote for *The Argus* doing around the grounds and he hated it, he didn't like watching Hawthorn playing St Kilda. He was a fair golfer, a two or three handicapper and he played district cricket as well.

Richo: Steve, tell us about your own footy and what led up to you playing that first game for the Dees in 1980. That would have been with Big Carl!

Stephen Bickford: My first game was out at VFL Park and it was Jezza's last game for St Kilda. I got there about two hours early and back in those days you rolled up in your sandshoes and jeans. I didn't have my pass so I said to the bloke on the gate, look, I'm playing in the main game, and he said, sure you are pal and I had to drive back home to get my pass and I was still half an hour early anyway. But Big Carl was great. I remember one game against Footscray and Carl, obviously being from St Kilda, and I was playing on Russell Tweeddale who'd played at St Kilda, too, and Russell was giving me the elbow before the game. So, Carl came up and pushed me away and then walked around the perimeter of the centre square with his arm around Russell Tweeddale just having a chat to him. Russell was walking along nodding at whatever Carl was saying and then didn't go near the ball all day.

Covey: That was an early version of unsociable football!

Stephen Bickford: Yeah, very much, but Carl was a great bloke and great to play with.

Billy: You wouldn't have had that problem at the gate if your debut had been at the MCG Stephen, they would have known you were George's boy!

Stephen Bickford: That's right. Actually, about eight years ago you did a segment about hack sons of Melbourne Football Club legends on your show and you were talking about David Cordner and myself. I was a guest in the committee room that day and I hadn't listened to your program on the way to the footy, so I walked into the committee room and Peter French and Stephen Gough burst out laughing. I said, 'What's happened?' and they said, 'Didn't you hear? They were bagging you on the Coodabeens today!'

Torch: That doesn't sound like us! Moving on... did George ever give you any advice about your football career?

Stephen Bickford: No, he used to come and watch but he didn't say a lot, he used to hide, I think. He was a bit underrated as a player, a lot of people thought he was one of the first six-foot centremen. He was very supportive but he didn't really give too much advice, he just enjoyed watching. The parents who get carried away are probably the ones that never really played the game.

Torch: The next year, after Big Carl, you had Barass, the prodigal son returning to Melbourne. How did you get on with Barass?

Stephen Bickford: Barass was pretty daunting, we were all in awe of him when he came along but we didn't have much of a list and obviously we were on the bottom. I played in that winning game out at the Bulldogs, the one game we won for the year in '81. We would be nine goals down at half-time and Barass would say, 'Guys if don't pull your finger out, you won't believe what training is gonna be like on Monday, Tuesday and Wednesday', and we'd all go in our shell a bit. He was obviously a great coach but I really enjoyed Slug, he was a great mentor. And Gags Gallagher, Hassa Mann, Stan Alves, all great names.

Champs: You mentioned that your father George retired at 25, but you were gone at 20, Stephen. What happened there?

Stephen Bickford: I struggled a bit in my second season, I only played the six games. I was the best first year player in '80 and then I was gone by '81.

Torch: Was it Barass who gave you the news?

Stephen Bickford: Yes, and in those days you got the flick on March 25 and the season was starting in two weeks' time so you didn't have much chance to do much more. And after that I played in the VFA at Prahran and then I played with Collegians from '86 and then I was chairman of selectors for Leigh Carlson who was coaching Collegians.

Richo: And you've kept up your involvement at the Melbourne footy club as well.

Stephen Bickford: I was on the board for nine years and luckily enough I was made a life member last year. I see a lot of the boys at different functions, I was at a life members' function where I saw Noel McMahon and Shane Zantuck and Steven Smith. I was very close with Robbie Flower, so that was a tragedy.

Covey: Did you did you play with Steven Smith?

Stephen Bickford: He said we were the slowest backline in the west. We had Robbie Elliot, Steve Smith and myself and a couple others so we weren't that quick but we had a good time.

Richo: Stephen, I want to finish on one question here. You're a life member of the club and you've been a board member. That jumper they wore last week. The away strip that looks like something you'd wear to training. Can we get rid of it, please?

Stephen Bickford: I hope so but the jumpers we wore were the royal blue because colour TV had just come in!

Richo: They look better.

Stephen Bickford: I don't know about that, I had a look at mine again the other day. I can't believe it doesn't fit me!

Richo: Stephen it's been wonderful talking to you this morning. Thank you so much.

Stephen Bickford: No worries fellas, cheers.

A Bag For The Blues

ROSS DITCHBURN

Ross Ditchburn wasn't recruited from the WAFL like most WA players to come over and try their luck in the VFL, he instead went to Carlton straight out of the bush, playing the '81 season for his hometown, Kukerin. And all Parko needed to convince him that Ross could be his next Premiership full forward was a recommendation from Ken Hunter and some scones from Ross' mum. Well it wasn't quite that simple, Ross came over as a centre half-forward for a start. And by July, he'd played just the single senior game.

Richo: Ross Ditchburn, welcome to the Coodabeens.

Ross Ditchburn: Good morning boys, how are you?

Richo: Ross, tell us about your move because you were one of those players who was going well in the WAFL and was signed to come to Victoria, but everyone was wondering whether you would ever come over. You must have been in your mid- to late-20s when you finally made the move?

Ross Ditchburn: I was 25 when I first went over, but I actually went from Kukerin, a little town in the wheatbelt, three hours south east of Perth. I'd left Claremont and had one year in the bush and I was recruited from Kukerin straight to Carlton.

Billy: Wow. Who was the person who finally persuaded you to come across?

Ross Ditchburn: David Parkin and Shane O'Sullivan caught a plane to Perth and jumped in a car and drove all the way down to Kukerin to see me on the strength of Kenny Hunter's recommendation. Mum cooked them up a feed of scones and they were very happy, so they were keen to get me over there because they thought if they did, they might get some more scones. I went over and watched the '81 Grand Final and met all the boys and thought that's the pinnacle, I'd love to be a part of it. And went over from there.

Richo: And when you first started you struggled in your first couple of games?

Ross Ditchburn: Well, yes, I did. They recruited me as a centre half-forward. And I used to avoid the weights at all costs, and probably wasn't strong enough to hold that position down. I remember going to Swan Hill on a plane to play a scratch match and when we took off from Essendon Airport they were taking some pens out of the plane and putting seats back, it was a bit of a hair-raising trip. But I managed to kick six goals that day, and that was just before the season started. I thought I was half a chance to play the first game, but that didn't happen. I didn't get a run until we played against Footscray about six weeks into the season and I was at centre half-forward. I think I got two kicks that day, and things didn't look too good at that stage. And it was then that I went and had a talk to David and said I don't think I can hold down centre half-forward and he said I don't think you can either, maybe we'll try you at full forward. So I played a couple of games in the ressies and kicked quite a few goals at full forward. And it seemed to suit me a lot better. And I never looked back from there. I think I kicked six against Melbourne and then 12 against St. Kilda in my first two games.

Champs: And as you said, you'd come over to watch the '81 Grand Final and that was enough to make you decide to make the move. Not many people play in a Premiership side in their first season.

Ross Ditchburn: No, I was very fortunate. And I know there were a lot of legendary AFL players that didn't ever play in a Grand Final. So I know how extremely lucky I was.

Covey: Of course this segment is called They Had Their Kicking Boots On and in Round 21, 1982 you had them on Ross because you kicked 9.2 against North. Have you got fond memories of that afternoon?

Ross Ditchburn: Yes, I've got fond memories of playing on David Dench. Denchy was one of those guys who was probably getting towards the end of his career. I played on a lot of guys that were getting towards the end of their careers back then. And a lot of them weren't used to leading full forwards. And the skill level of the players I had in front of me was just outstanding, I only had to have a couple yards on my opponent and they would put it down my throat. And I was fortunate that I was a reasonably straight shot for goal.

Covey: And with apologies I should say I overlooked the fact that five weeks earlier against St Kilda in Round 16 you kicked 12.2! 12 kicks and 13 marks!

Ross Ditchburn: I remember that day because I had 12 and Mike Fitzpatrick ran past me and I thought jeepers, he's the skipper, I've got to look after him. So I've handballed it over the top and I've hit him in the back of the head. He said, 'You're the first full forward that's ever handballed the ball!' He said I should have kicked the 13 and that would have equalled the Carlton goalkicking record. But anyway, I was thrilled to be a part of that era. They were a team of legends and I still keep in touch with them all now and we have some great times together.

Billy: You certainly had your kicking boots on for that whole 1982 season you kick 61 goals and only 20 behinds. Was goalkicking a big part of your training regime?

Ross Ditchburn: It certainly was. We were allowed to stay out after training and shoot for goal for 20 minutes or whatever we needed to do. And you could also do a bit before training as well. It's so structured and regimented now that they probably don't allow the blokes that opportunity. Because if they're not supervised they might get injured and it's just a completely different ball game these days. I think it was probably a better spectacle back in our day with the contest. You've certainly got to be an athlete to play these days but the skill level when they're shooting for goal is not where it should be. But they do seem to be able to pinpoint the targets around the ground.

Torch: You kept playing footy until you were 38, what was your best bag anywhere anytime?

Ross Ditchburn: Ah 23.2, Kukerin versus Dumbleyung at Stubbs Park in Dumbleyung.

Billy: At what age was that?

Ross Ditchburn: That was when I had retired from Carlton and gone back to my hometown and I played for another 10 years when I got back home.

Champs: So what happened with the two points?

Ross Ditchburn: The goal umpire got it wrong! It did go through. But another day in a second semi-final against Narrogin at Darkan, I kicked 16 goals straight and we came down from about eight goals down at half-time to win by a couple of goals.

Billy: Your boy coaches Kukerin currently, doesn't he?

Ross Ditchburn: He does coach Kukerin. And last year, I coached the D grade because I've got a younger boy as well. And he's now at Aquinas College. going very well with his footy and he's in a development squad at South Fremantle. I've had a lot of fun out of watching my boys play footy and Nathan played

10 games for Peel when my brother was coaching down there, and Troy played 30 games for South Fremantle. So they're all happy in life, and I am as well.

Billy: And that's all that matters isn't it?

Covey: You told us earlier that you got picked up at the airport. But the boot's on the other foot today?

Ross Ditchburn: Exactly. I'm off to the airport this morning to pick up David Parkin and take him down to Kulin. And there's a group of guys running 1500km raising awareness of prostate cancer and men's health issues. And David's kindly donated his time to be involved with that. He'll have his lycra on and he's going to ride the bike with the boys for the last couple of hours when they run into Kulin today. He's then taking a coaching session, and he'll be the guest speaker at the function tonight. We really appreciate that he's doing that for us. And tomorrow night we've got Ross Glendinning and Bruce Yardley in Kukerin for a similar sort of function so it should be a couple of big nights.

Covey: Well we better come over there one day and you can talk us through the 23.2 and the 16 straight!

Ross Ditchburn: That'd be awesome.

Torch: Are you still following the Blues?

Ross Ditchburn: Yeah, still following the Blues and I was as disappointed as anything the other night when they could not kick a goal to get over the line.

Torch: One bright light would have been to see Jimmy Buckley's boy Dylan running around because he played pretty well.

Ross Ditchburn: Yeah. And I was listening to Sellers doing the commentary and he was biased! Because he and Jimmy Buckley are very good mates and I thought he was very biased about Jimmy's son. But he's obviously a real terrier Dylan and I hope he gets plenty more opportunities and really makes his mark at Carlton.

Richo: He was among the best. Ross, it has been wonderful talking to you. Thank you so much.

Ross Ditchburn: No problem fellas and keep up the good work. We listen to your program over here and you just do a fantastic job and keep those hits coming out!

Champs: Thanks Ross.

Richo: Ross Ditchburn. he kicked 23 goals in two games!

Covey: 12.2 against the Saints and 9.2 against the Kangas.

Richo: And he only played the two years before going back to look after the farm.

DARYL GILMORE

Bendigo boy Daryl Gilmore lived the dream of playing in the Big Smoke when he made his debut for Carlton in Round 4, 1983. The dream got even better when he kicked a goal with his first kick before finishing with three majors for the afternoon. In one of football's great mysteries, Daryl was dropped after this promising start and did not play another senior game. He revealed his befuddlement during a chat in 2015.

Torch: G'day Daryl. Are you one of those many players who came down to Carlton from Bendigo?

Daryl Gilmore: That's right. Yeah.

Richo: Let's go back to Round 4, 1983 and the realisation of a dream. You're running out for your first game with Carlton. Tell us how it went.

Daryl Gilmore: Well, it was a big, big day for me to be honest. The night before I actually worked in a sports store up in Bendigo and we used to work 9am to 9pm on the Friday nights with the late-night shopping. And I get a call on the phone at about seven o'clock and my boss said David Parkin's on the phone and I just thought it was someone messing around. I knew I was in and picked as 19th man and I knew that I was playing but it was David on the phone and he said you're actually starting so we want you down tonight. So, I knocked off at nine o'clock and drove down. They put me in the motel across the road from the footy oval and I don't remember a lot about that night because I didn't sleep too well. I tossed and turned but it was a fantastic day. I always barracked for Melbourne ever since I was a young fellow and to play against Melbourne in my first and only game was a big thrill.

Richo: Tell us about the first kick.

Daryl Gilmore: I remember big Warren Jones, big Wow, he got the ball from around the middle. He kicked it down towards me. I led out and took a bit of a chest mark, went back 35 metres out—or it might have been 135—but I think it was only 35.

Covey: Were you kicking to the Heatley Stand end or the scoreboard end?

Daryl Gilmore: It was the scoreboard end. And it went straight.

Billy: You were playing full forward Daryl, who were you playing on?

Daryl Gilmore: I played on Steven Smith.

Covey: We had him on last week. And if only we'd known, we would have asked about that game he played on you.

Daryl Gilmore: He probably wouldn't remember that, to be honest.

Richo: He should remember it because he didn't concede just the one goal, did he?

Daryl Gilmore: No, no, that's true. Yeah, I ended up kicking three for the day. And I regret now I should have had four because I did handball one which I didn't do often but Bruce Reid was in the goal square and I was only about 15 metres out and I popped it over top and he kicked it. So, I should have had 4.1 that day.

GILMORE, WE'VE GOT YOU STARTING ON TOMORROW!
FRANKLY GILMORE, I THOUGHT YOU'D BE A BIT MORE EXCITED.
HARV

Covey: We've got you down for five kicks and you've kicked 3.1 and given one away. You've been pretty productive.

Daryl Gilmore: It was wet, too, it was slippery and wet and Carlton had a few injuries at the time. And there were a few players who only had half a dozen games behind them as well. Melbourne threw everything at us and we ended up getting home by about 13 points, I think, so it was a really good victory.

Covey: And when you went in the rooms to sing the song, because it was your first game, did they put you in the middle of the circle and pour soft drink over you?

Daryl Gilmore: No, we didn't do that back then. I didn't know some of the words but it did bring a tear to the eye.

Billy: What happened for Round 5? I reckon three goals and an assist would've got you in the starting 20 for the next week.

Daryl Gilmore: To be honest, I really don't know. But I think the biggest reason was that at the time they had a very good full forward and a really good side, you know, they had players like Peter Bosustow and Ross Ditchburn.

Covey: None of them kicked a goal with their first kick and you had three out of five. I mean, it's a mystery to you and it's a mystery to us, too, Daryl. We run into Parko a bit, has he ever explained it to you?

Daryl Gilmore: I actually heard I was dropped. I heard it on the radio on a Thursday night because I used to travel down only on the Tuesday to train and I'd train back up here with Eaglehawk on the Thursday night and then I'd stay down Saturday night to train on Sunday, but I didn't know I was dropped until I heard the league teams on the radio, to be honest.

Richo: So, there wasn't another 7pm call to the sports shop from Parko?

Daryl Gilmore: I missed out on that one.

Covey: Did you come down the next week and play in the reserves?

Daryl Gilmore: Yeah, I did. Played reserves all season.

Covey: Didn't Parko talk to you at all?

Daryl Gilmore: Not really. I went downhill after that game, I lost a bit of confidence as the season went on.

Covey: Here was a time when, you know, blokes like Steven Oliver were reluctant to come down. And you've come down for your first game of footy...

Richo: On two hours' notice...

Covey: On Steven Smith one of the great full backs of all time. What's going on?

Daryl Gilmore: I'm still waiting for the call. I might get the call next week.

Richo: I think that's when the rot set in at Carlton. People talk about the Norm Smith thing at Melbourne, they should be talking about the Daryl Gilmore thing at Carlton.

Covey: Did you kick a few in the reserves for the rest of the year?

Daryl Gilmore: Not a great deal. For the first three rounds, I was on fire. I was going really well. The week before I got the senior game we played out at Waverley and it was a real windy, wet, old day. I kicked 10.1 against Collingwood.

Richo: Who was the full back that day?

Daryl Gilmore: I'm not sure but I think it was Neil Peart an ex-Richmond player. He was gonna kill me that day. Every time

I got near the ball, it just fell into my arms. I was lucky and he was gonna murder me! Some of the things he said to me were not nice.

Covey: We've unearthed one of football's great mysteries here.

Daryl Gilmore: Look, it was a great experience. I suppose I was a country boy and I didn't know my way around Melbourne too well and things like that. So, it was always a bit of a drama to get to a ground, find the ground and find the directions and get there on time and things like that.

Covey: Did you go back to Bendigo then the next year?

Daryl Gilmore: I stayed down. I did a pre-season. I actually was lucky enough to get a trip to Hawaii on the pre-season camp. When I stepped off the plane to be picked up, no one recognised me! I'd lost that much weight, they trained the living daylights out of us.

Billy: You're an Eaglehawk boy?

Daryl Gilmore: No, I played with Eaglehawk. But I started in the Heathcote league, I was a Tooborac boy.

Richo: Daryl, it's a sensational story. A goal with your first kick in your first game, kicking three goals for the game and that ending up being your only senior game. Extraordinary.

Covey: We're all wondering why Daryl never got a second game!

Daryl Gilmore: Look, David Parkin did say to me, he said don't go back to Bendigo with a big head. You played really well but you never had one tackle.

Covey: Did you kick a few when you went back home?

Daryl Gilmore: 120-odd the next year. Yeah, so I kicked a lot of goals over the time.

Covey: When you kicked the 120, did any other clubs have a nibble to try and get you to come back down?

Daryl Gilmore: When I went back I actually could have gone to Melbourne if I wanted to and I had a bit of interest from Collingwood as well. Look, I was a country boy and I decided to come and play back at Eaglehawk and, yeah, I enjoyed my footy up there and they were a great club to me. I had a lot of years up there so what you miss out sometimes you pick up in other ways.

Torch: Do you catch up with any of those players you played with at Carlton these days, Daryl?

Daryl Gilmore: I don't see many. I actually I did get invited to the 150-year celebration a few months ago and that was really good. And I did catch up with a lot of the reserves players and a few of the senior players and I actually congratulated big Wow because he was the guy who kicked the ball to me.

Richo: Well it is a team game.

Daryl Gilmore: Wow loved it. He didn't remember it but he said he'll take it!

Richo: And Daryl, you still follow the Dees in your heart of hearts?

Daryl Gilmore: Look I love Melbourne. I still follow Carlton a little bit, but I've strayed a bit towards the Western Bulldogs now. They're a great club and they've got some great young players down there and I reckon the Bulldogs will be on the rise in a couple of years' time.

Richo: Daryl, thanks again. It's been wonderful talking to you this morning.

Daryl Gilmore: No worries at all.

Torch: I did a coaching course many years ago and Parko was

one of the guest speakers. And he said he was the first coach to ring every player on a Friday night before the game except one.

Richo: Two innovations: one is going crook at the full forward because he kicked too many goals and didn't do any tackles and the other one's ringing blokes up and telling them that they're in the team. Very good!

WARREN RALPH

The early 1980s was a time when every second full forward in the VFL seemed to have come out of Western Australia. And Claremont's Warren Ralph certainly burst onto the scene when he crossed to Carlton in 1984 on what ended up being the league's last Form 4 transfer. Ralph kicked nine and picked up two Brownlow votes in the first of a career that spanned just 21 VFL games.

Richo: Warren Ralph, welcome to the Coodabeens.

Warren Ralph: Morning, gents.

Richo: Tell us the whole story of the Form 4 and how Carlton managed to snag you.

Warren Ralph: Obviously the biggest part of a Form 4 was that they gave you some cash up front.

Covey: Were they allowed to Warren?

Warren Ralph: I think that was the old Form 4 rules, wasn't it? It was my belief was that whoever came with the Form 4 and had the biggest dollar in their hand, generally got the signature. So yeah, I signed up for a few dollars, and due to the old taxation laws in those days I didn't have to pay tax on it. So that was even better.

Champs: A Form 4 was a mythical thing to us, but did you bother to ask what a form one, two or three looks like?

Warren Ralph: It didn't come into my head when they put a cheque in my hand!

Richo: So at that stage, you had established yourself as a player in the WAFL, you were 25, which clubs had had a go at getting you over to Melbourne?

Warren Ralph: Carlton was really the only club. Melbourne had approached me and said they were going to get me in the first draft, which was going to happen the following year in '81. But because there was no guarantee you're going to that club in the draft, I thought, look, Carlton are a pretty good side, they've won a couple of Premierships and were very successful. So that just put the icing on the cake that I was going to a pretty successful club.

Covey: And who would have thought that when you then saddled up for Round 1, 30 years ago this round, that you'd kick nine goals. Were you feeling pretty good going into the game?

Warren Ralph: Oh yeah, I was because of the team I was in, the players in front of me were pretty good. The likes of Buckley, Johnston, Ashman, Sheldon, Glascott and the list goes on. And playing at Waverley probably suited me more than anything because it was similar to the grounds over here. Long, wide open spaces which suited my sort of game. And I just had a day in the park.

Torch: And what was the biggest bag you'd kicked in a game playing for Claremont before you came over?

Warren Ralph: Sixteen against Subi. It was actually the year before I came to Carlton.

Champs: Where there other big scores apart from the 16?

Warren Ralph: I had a few 11s, some 10s and so on. So that was obviously the biggest but yeah, I've kicked double figures. I couldn't tell you how many times but it has happened.

Billy: It's a wonder more clubs didn't come after you after you've kicked 16. This is surprising.

Warren Ralph: As you guys have said I signed the last Form 4 available. So whether the clubs had used them prior I don't know. But as I said I was approached and I signed on the dotted line.

Richo: Warren that first year at Carlton you played 14 games and kicked 55.33 which is a fabulous return. But then after that you had another couple of years but you hardly played any games at all. What happened?

Warren Ralph: I missed all of '85 with a knee injury. I busted my knee in the first home and away game and then played the last home and away game in the reserves. And then in '86 Robert Walls came to the club and we didn't see eye to eye to be honest. So that was sort of the end of it.

Torch: After you finished at Carlton did you go back to WA?

Warren Ralph: Yeah I came back here. I played with Claremont, played in a couple of Premierships in '87 and '89 and hung up the boots at the ripe age of 30.

Champs: Now, Warren, we can ask you this because no one in Perth will be listening, are you Eagles or Dockers?

Warren Ralph: Carlton. It's funny guys and it's not like I want to sound corny or anything, but it's in your blood when you go to the Blues. They are a very good club. When I come to Melbourne and I try to get to the Collingwood-Carlton game once a year, I always get tickets from the club.

Covey: Let me go back to when you first started, and you kicked nine that first week against North, you kicked six the next week against Fitzroy so you were on fire early weren't you?

Warren Ralph: I had a pretty good start. The six was at the old Junction Oval. Again, a reasonably big ground. I just started off well but after that I had a few injury problems. I popped my shoulder halfway through the year so you know, 14 games wasn't too bad. But the only downside about being at Carlton was the ground. Princes Park was probably not suited to my style of football being a little bit smaller, it didn't really adhere to my style of game. But once I got out on the bigger grounds like Waverley or the MCG, that suited my play.

Covey: My memory might be fading but did you have a big game one day at Waverley against Collingwood it might have been an Anzac Day match in front of a huge crowd?

Warren Ralph: Well it wasn't a big day in terms of goals. It was when I supposedly kicked the point on the siren that could have drawn the game. That was Anzac Day, '84. When the goal umpire slipped and it actually went through the goals and Jimmy Buckley did a Rex Hunt on the goal line, and then the goal umpire pulled out one finger and we lost by five points. So that's probably not my fondest memory.

Covey: But that would have been the biggest crowd you'd played in front of I'd reckon.

Warren Ralph: Oh, yeah, absolutely. In the '81 Grand Final over here there was just over 50,000 and in State of Origin games over here we'd get 45-50,000, but you're going out on Anzac Day in front of 74-75,000 people and when I ran out onto the ground I had goosebumps.

Champs: Warren looking at today's footy with 18 clubs, which of the big marking, goal-kicking forwards going around do you like at the moment?

Warren Ralph: I don't know if there's a true big marking forward. I think it's more an athlete's game now, I just think you have to be an athlete before you're a footballer. Matthew Pavlich is obviously a big strong marking forward and Jeremy Cameron from GWS is a future star of the game. But I don't think there's going to be your Locketts or Dunstalls anymore because they're a different type of footballer to what is going around at the moment. If you're a key forward these days, you probably have to be about six-foot six, six-foot seven. Whereas the old six-foot three full forward is probably playing on a wing or half-back flank.

Richo: Warren, it's been terrific talking to you this morning. Thank you so much.

Warren Ralph: Not a problem.

Richo: Warren Ralph. The man who came over on a Form 4 and kicked a bag in his first game for Carlton.

Better At The Same Age

DEAN HARDING

With pick 79 in the 1990 AFL national draft, Essendon selected a young blond-headed half-forward flanker from Canberra by the name of James Hird. The pick prior, No 78, was held by Fitzroy and they used it on a kid from Wangaratta named Dean Harding. Harding went on to play 19 games for the Lions between 1991 and '93.

Covey: Dean Harding, welcome to the Coodabeens.

Dean Harding: G'day guys, how are we going?

Covey: You're the first pick 78 we've had on the show.

Dean Harding: Thank you mate, pleased to be on.

Richo: Now you were picked by Fitzroy, did you have any connection with Fitzroy at all beforehand? Had they spoken to you at all?

Dean Harding: No, not really back in those days. You got the odd letter from a club every now and then and that was about it. I don't think I spoke to anyone at that stage.

Covey: In 1990, the draft wasn't the media event it is now. Can you recall how you were informed that you'd been chosen?

Dean Harding: I think it was a phone call from a mate who'd heard it on the radio. I might have been at the Pinsent Hotel in Wangaratta at the time.

Billy: You would have just turned 18 and been allowed into a hotel.

Dean Harding: Exactly. Yeah. Exactly.

Covey: Pinsent Hotel. We went there a couple years ago.

Dean Harding: Yeah, I think Crusher and the boys probably think I'm about 50 given I've been going there for so long.

Champs: So you're a Wang boy obviously.

Dean Harding: Correct. Born and bred Wangaratta.

Richo: Did any of your teammates or opponents in footy around Wangaratta get drafted that year?

Dean Harding: That year before, Naishy got drafted to Richmond. I grew up with Naishy, he went to Wangaratta and I went to Rovers. A couple of years after me, Luke Norman went down to Melbourne. We had a really strong connection earlier with North Melbourne as well with Darren Steele and Paul Bryce and a heap of others but that was a few years earlier than me.

Covey: As a country boy from Wang you would have felt pretty much at home in Fitzroy because they always struck us as being like a country footy club in the city.

Dean Harding: I was probably a bit taken aback when I got there. I reckon the facilities at the Rovers were better than the ones down at the Lakeside Oval.

Torch: And who was coaching when you went down there?

Dean Harding: We had Rob Shaw who'd just finished a stint with Essendon over with Sheeds and he'd come in. He was going to fix everything up at Fitzroy. But three years later, I think he was done as well.

Covey: And so you played three seasons '91, '92 and '93. I don't think James played his first game till '93.

Dean Harding: Yeah, I always told my mates that Essendon was filthy that they missed out on me!

Billy: Well, James Hird was just wiling away his time in the magoos for three years while you were playing for Fitzroy. One thing with your Fitzroy career that I can't recall or understand looking at your stats. You played 12 games in your first season 1991, only the two games in '92 and yet in those two games, Fitzroy won both the games you kicked goals in, so what was going on in '92?

Dean Harding: I don't know what was going on, maybe Shawry and the crew got it wrong, I'm not sure. But I had a lot of injuries to hamstrings and thighs. I think back in those days, the science behind training wasn't up to speed and we just trained as hard as we could every night and morning. I suppose my body couldn't put up with it at that stage, so I didn't get through much footy after that.

Covey: So while your body might have let you down, did you enjoy your time in Melbourne coming down from the bush?

Dean Harding: I absolutely loved it. It was probably pretty daunting at the start. But as you're settling into a footy club, you get to know a heap of the boys and like you said it was a big country footy club. You had Doc Wheildon and those sort of boys around so it was always an enjoyable place to be.

Torch: And you would have had Alistair Lynch there too?

Dean Harding: Yeah, big Al was there with Roosy and Richard Osborne, and Matty Armstrong.

Richo: Graham Osborne?

Dean Harding: No he'd left the year before, I inherited his number actually. We had Jimmy Wynd he was a little star and big Johnny Ironmonger and James Manson came across so we had a pretty good crew.

Torch: And you were playing your home games at Princes Park in those days?

Dean Harding: Yeah Princes Park was fantastic and we actually used to knock off the odd decent side occasionally at Princes Park which was always good fun.

Torch: I remember, I think against North and John McCarthy stitched up Wayne Carey, you had a great day and that would have been in the early '90s too I think.

Dean Harding: Yeah it was, I played that day. McCarthy was built up all week because he obviously crossed from North Melbourne to us. So Shawry built him up all week and he came out and did the job on Wayne and I think we ended up winning by two or three points that day, so it was a good one. We certainly enjoyed our wins boys, that was for sure. Now, that might have been the problem. I think every win was like a Premiership and we definitely excelled in that area.

Richo: You played an exciting brand of footy and your three seasons '91, '92, '93 —pick 78 in the draft was looking okay. And then all of a sudden James Hird came from the clouds pick 79.

Dean Harding: He did! He sort of took over. And Essendon might have been thinking that they'd made the right choice again.

Champs: And what about yourself Dean, after you finished up with Fitzroy, what have you done in footy?

Dean Harding: Yeah, I moved back closer to home. I was

umming and ahing at that stage about whether to go across to SA, Port Adelaide was still in the SANFL at that stage and I nearly went across there but in the end I wanted to come back closer to home. I ended up in Wodonga which is probably 45 minutes down the road from Wang and transferred with work and played here. I was going to stay a year, get redrafted and go back, and 23 or 24 years later, I'm still here.

Richo: And you're currently coaching Wodonga in the O and M is that right?

Dean Harding: Yeah, that's right. Ever since I got here in '94 I've been involved. There was one year I snuck out to Rutherglen and coached but other than that, I've been involved with the footy club ever since. And this is my second year coaching the senior boys.

Billy: And how's it going for you?

Dean Harding: We got belted last week, Myrtleford got hold of us. They had three or four boys off their VFL list available and they certainly gave us a bit of a towelling and showed us how to go about it. But the boys are going along OK, I'm just standing out on the ground at the moment and it looks an absolute picture and the boys are getting organised for a big day against Corowa.

Covey: Well if you get any of those young fellas who think they know better than the coach and they act like upstarts just pull them into line Dean and say, listen, mate, I was picked ahead of James Hird in the draft.

Dean Harding: I might try that one but then I'll have to say who I played for and when I say Fitzroy, half of them won't know who that is!

Richo: Dean, obviously your main commitment and involvement is at Wodonga footy club but at the AFL level, how have you managed your loyalties?

Dean Harding: Yes, initially I probably just kept following the boys. There were obviously a few still playing so you keep following. After that, I probably went back to Hawthorn because I was a Hawthorn follower as a kid, so I had it pretty good growing up. But then obviously the Brisbane boys won those flags and I got a few free tickets so I jumped back on that wagon and watched a few Grand Finals and my young bloke who's 10 now keeps asking if he's allowed to change sides, but I've got him on the Brisbane Lions as well.

Billy: You can't change sides! So you're a Lions family.

Dean Harding: My young bloke and I are, my wife's Collingwood so we won't talk about that and my daughter is Geelong.

Champs: You're in a mixed household Dean which is difficult I know, but you've got to look forward to the Lions-Collingwood game coming up so that'll be fun.

Dean Harding: It's not too bad to be honest. My wife thinks Daicos and all those blokes are still playing!

Richo: Dean, it's been terrific talking to you this morning. You've obviously got work to do there at the footy ground today. So have a fantastic day and a fantastic season.

Dean Harding: Thanks, guys. Thanks for having me.

Richo: Dean Harding pick 78 in the 1990 national draft. Pick 79 was James Hird.

ANDREW GRIBBLE

One of the most famous picks in the history of the draft was Chris Grant (Footscray) who was selected at No. 105 in 1988. Famous because of how late he went and the fact that he became a champion at the Bulldogs playing 350 games, captaining the club and being inducted into the Australian Football Hall of Fame in 2012. If that's what you get at 105, then Geelong must have been excited about securing Andrew Gribble at No. 104.

Andrew Gribble: Gentlemen, how are we?

Richo: Good thanks, Andrew. Now, the draft was still a very new thing back in 1988, wasn't it?

Andrew Gribble: It was, I'd never heard of it until the night before the '88 draft.

Richo: You'd never heard of it but you were in it. How did that work out?

Andrew Gribble: I'd never had any interest in it. I got a phone call from Billy McMaster the night before and he made a suggestion that he thought they might draft me the next day. And I thought that sounds like a good idea and I said yes to the idea.

Billy: Where were you playing at the time?

Andrew Gribble: I was drafted from St Peters in the GFL.

Torch: Didn't you have to put in some paperwork to be in the draft?

Andrew Gribble: Not back then.

Covey: Where'd you go to school, Andrew?

Andrew Gribble: I actually grew up in Swan Hill, Ian.

Covey: So how did you end up at St Peter's?

Andrew Gribble: I went down to uni. Geelong had actually got me down there two years earlier and I was going to play in the Under 19s and I went and had a look at that. There were about 120 kids there and I ran the other way. I wasn't a footballer, I came from a basketball background. I'd never played junior footy and I was a basketballer 365 days of the year.

Covey: So, you told us that Bill McMaster said that they were looking at drafting you. How did you find out you'd actually been drafted? Because I don't reckon it was on the telly back then.

Andrew Gribble: They rang me and then I read about it in the paper the next day.

Richo: So, you'd never heard of the draft. And obviously you'd never heard of Chris Grant either.

Andrew Gribble: No, I hadn't. It's my trivia question in life when people find out that I was drafted in '88 and went at 104, I usually tell them that between me and pick 105 we played 350 quality games!

Billy: Tell us about the first night you went to training at the Cats, Andrew.

Andrew Gribble: Look, because of my lack of football background, it was all a little bit overwhelming to me. If you'd picked me up and dumped me onto the court at the Melbourne Tigers I would have felt a lot more comfortable, knowing my way around the basketball court. But I didn't think I was much of a footballer to be honest. Having only really played for maybe four years from 17 years old onwards, so it was a little bit daunting and I probably went through the whole year a little bit intimidated without any ambition. You were expected to do what you did and there was never any development that went along with it back then. You probably put as much into it then as what local GFL footballers put into their craft these days.

Covey: It was Malcolm Blight's first year and there was a lot of excitement about Malcolm being down at the club for '89, wasn't there?

Andrew Gribble: It was a hell of a year, '89. The thirds or the Under 19s at the time, the seconds and the senior team all played in the Grand Final and they lost by a combined nine points. And it really was the year of the Gary Ablett show. I do remember as the year progressed there was a race to the showers and a race to get out and see what Gary was gonna do that day.

Torch: How did your first season start, Andrew?

Andrew Gribble: I rolled an ankle playing basketball and so I missed the first couple of weeks of the season proper.

Richo: Malcom Blight became legendary for his unusual approach to football and coaching. What was your experience of Blighty as a coach?

Andrew Gribble: I think I spoke to him twice! And I think one of those times was when he picked me up at the gate as I was walking from Noble Street into the ground. He picked me up and took me the rest of the way so that was one of the two times he spoke to me. Blighty was very eccentric. And look, it was a year where I think they turned over about 26 players in the senior team.

Richo: And Andrew how did your footy career pan out and what has your involvement in footy been since?

Andrew Gribble: I started up in Swan Hill and in my HSC a neighbour of mine, who was coaching Swan Hill at the time, said I want you to play footy this year and I still played basketball but I put it to the side and I spent two years there. I played a year at Torquay when I came down originally to Geelong for the Under 19s and then St Peters. I went to Geelong for the year and I probably really didn't enjoy it that much, I had basketball instincts and was a bit of an athlete and I knew very little about football. I left Geelong after that. I probably made up my mind that it wasn't for me about halfway through the year. I went to West Adelaide for two years, probably started to get the game a little bit there. I came back and when to South Barwon for a couple of years, primarily because I knew Michael Crutchfield who was coaching. I then went back to Geelong West-St Peters and retired in '98 at the ripe old age of 29.

Covey: There's a boy named Michael Luxford who has come to Geelong from basketball and they've talked about how they're going to try and turn him into a footballer. I hope people realise he's actually the Andrew Gribble of the current day.

Andrew Gribble: I can certainly see the appeal of basketballers within football. If I had any strength it was the ability to make a decision in close.

Richo: A lot of basketball is played in close even though it's meant to be a non-contact sport.

Covey: Exactly what Scott Pendlebury does.

Richo: Andrew, fascinating talking with you this morning, and everyone now knows who was picked at 104 in the 1988 national draft.

Andrew Gribble passed away in November 2020 after a battle with cancer. He was 53. One of his former coaches, Darrell Fenton, described Gribble as 'a bloody good player... and I'm not exaggerating that. He was such a star.'

ROB MALONE

When Hawthorn called out the name Shane Crawford at pick 13 in the 1991 national draft, could they have known they had a 300-game Premiership player on their hands? And if so, what did St Kilda think when they took young West Australian Rob Malone with the pick prior? Rob didn't manage a senior game for the Saints in two years at Linton Street but went on to run West Perth in the WAFL and eventually moved across the ditch to run footy in New Zealand.

Richo: Rob Malone, good morning.

Rob Malone: G'day boys, how are you?

Richo: Can we wind the clock back to the 1991 draft? Have you got any memory of it at all?

Rob Malone: It was a long time ago but I do. I played at Claremont in the WAFL under Gerard Neesham and we had a pretty good season in '91 winning the Premiership, and seven out of the first 12 picked were Claremont players. So it was very exciting to make the move to Melbourne for the '92 season.

Richo: So did you have a sense that you might be picked? Had St Kilda talked to you beforehand?

Rob Malone: Yes, it was John Beveridge with Ken Sheldon and Peter Hudson.

Champs: Who did you barrack for in the AFL at the time?

Rob Malone: I actually barracked for St Kilda, I had a Trevor Barker jumper as a kid. I couldn't get off the ground like him, but I thought he was a pretty special player.

Champs: Did you meet Barks when you came over?

Rob Malone: I worked at his gym for about two weeks. He had a gym in Sandringham and I was his cleaner, I lasted about 10 days.

Billy: Barks didn't sack you did he?

Rob Malone: It was probably by mutual agreement. I'd have to get up at 5.30 and Barks would wander in with at about 9 o'clock.

Torch: You weren't the only Malone who tried his luck in the AFL were you Rob?

Rob Malone: No, one of my brothers, Jim Malone, was the CEO at Richmond.

Richo: Wow, I know Jim well.

Rob Malone: I actually spoke to him this morning and he said to say g'day to you Richo.

Richo: Terrific, g'day back to good old Jim. Rob, tell us about the astonishing Claremont connection in that draft. Which of your other teammates from Claremont were drafted in the same draft as you?

Rob Malone: John Hutton, Phil Gilbert, Andrew McGovern, Darren Kowal who played for Melbourne.

Covey: I'll give you a hand here, Rob. John Hutton was No. 1. Darren Kowal, three, Andrew McGovern at four, Jason Norrish at five. Paul Burton who went to Sydney at six, Jeremy Guard at seven. And then you've come through at 12. And then a bit further down the list is Phil Gilbert at 19.

Rob Malone: And there was also Brendan Barrows at about 80 who went to Collingwood, and I lived with him in Melbourne.

Richo: Tell us about walking into St Kilda for the first time.

Rob Malone: It was interesting. My oldest brother David came with me and we walked into the old Moorabbin in Linton Street and the first person we bumped into was Tony Lockett. And he didn't say anything to me he just grunted and said get out of my way. And the second person I met was Peter Hudson, who was an assistant coach with Ken Sheldon.

Champs: He would be entirely opposite to Plugger in his PR.

Rob Malone: Huddo was reasonably ruthless but a good guy. I really liked Ken Sheldon and St Kilda was a great club but in those days, the set up and change rooms were pretty primitive.

Richo: That's extraordinary Rob you come all the way across the country to play footy and the first two people you meet are probably the two greatest full forwards in the history of the game!

Rob Malone: I ended up idolising Plugger and I trained and played with Harvey and Winmar. And those guys were extraordinary. It was a good experience but unfortunately it was pretty short-lived.

Covey: And so you didn't crack it for a game Rob.

Rob Malone: I played five Foster's Cup games but I was there for two seasons and it was pretty hard to break into the mid-field with Harvey, Winmar, Burke, Devonport, Greig, they had a pretty good side. I struggled but I played for two years in the twos. I've got a number of nephews who are big on the AFL stats and they always give me a hard time because the only thing I had in common with Shane Crawford who played about 800 games was that I went to Marist Brothers and he went to Assumption College and that was where the similarity ended.

Billy: Have you ever met Shane Crawford?

Rob Malone: No, I haven't.

Covey: It's a long way from Perth to Melbourne and now you're in New Zealand. Did you get picked up in the New Zealand draft?

Rob Malone: I would have been No. 1 pick in the New Zealand draft. I married a Kiwi, Amy, and I have a son here and live in Auckland. I actually went over there originally when I was the CEO at West Perth footy club. The AFL had an office in New Zealand and were trying to grow the game here and I moved over in January 2004 to run the New Zealand AFL and we started with two people and now they've got a staff of about 50 people.

Torch: How many teams are running around over there?

Rob Malone: To put it into context, they have a league in Auckland of six clubs, a league in Christchurch of four clubs, a league in Waikato, a league in Dunedin and a league in Wellington. They all play their own competitions and they play outside the rugby season, which is a protected species. So from September, October through to Christmas, they play the footy season here. And then they play a provincial championship and then the national team is picked out of that and I coach the national team.

Billy: Rob you said you play Australian football sensibly at a different time in the calendar to the rugby season over there in

New Zealand. Do you get much crossover of people who are rugby players who give footy a crack?

Rob Malone: It's a good question and they do. The AFL has done really well at offering an alternative sport to the First 15 schools. First 15 rugby is big business, it's on TV and it's the big schools who play. The AFL takes the backs who are the outside guys who run the ball in rugby and they teach them how to get off the ground which is foreign territory for rugby players. And they probably get one in 10 guys who will convert from rugby to Aussie Rules.

Richo: Rob, it's been wonderful talking to you this morning. Thank you so much.

Rob Malone: Good to chat to you guys. Thanks very much for your time.

Richo: No worries. Rob Malone drafted by St Kilda at pick 12 in the '91 draft. Extraordinary because the next pick was Shane Crawford.

BEN MOORE

AFL games record holder Brent 'Boomer' Harvey was taken at pick 47 by North Melbourne in the 1995 national draft. One spot ahead of him at No. 46, Richmond selected Ben Moore who went on to play 24 games for the Tigers, just 408 fewer than Harvey. He later captained Glenelg in the SANFL.

Richo: Ben Moore, welcome to the Coodabeens.

Ben Moore: Thank you. Thanks for having me on.

Richo: How well do you remember draft night way back then?

Ben Moore: It's a long time ago, but I still remember getting the opportunity to play for the Tigers, so good memories from back then.

Richo: And by pick 46, it's going on a bit, were you starting to wonder whether you're gonna get picked at all?

Ben Moore: Well, that's exactly right, there's no guarantees in the draft scenario, but you look through the past and there's always some decent ones who get picked up fairly late in the piece.

Covey: Had Richmond spoken to you?

Ben Moore: I think I'd had a quick chat to them at the time beforehand. And they said there were no guarantees but they were interested and if the opportunity arose, would you come over? And, of course, you say yes.

Richo: And then the very next pick after you, 47, was Brent Harvey. Had you encountered him at all in junior footy?

Ben Moore: No, I hadn't because I think he's a Melbourne boy.

Richo: So you hadn't seen him in Teal Cup or anything?

Ben Moore: Nothing at all. I hadn't come across him but we had a few encounters over my four years odd at Richmond. He was always a step above me, mate. He was a good little player.

Billy: Who was coaching at Richmond the four years you were there, Ben?

Ben Moore: They changed a bit. We had Robert Walls to start with which was nice as a young fella coming in and getting a fairly hard coach like Wallsy. And then Jeff Gieschen took over for the last couple of years I was there.

Billy: You got about four games that first year with the Tiges. Did Wallsy offer you instruction about how to find your feet in the modern game?

Ben Moore: One thing with Wallsy was he was very honest. So you knew where you stood with him. And you knew exactly what you needed to do if you wanted a game. So as a young fella, just battling away it was nice to know exactly what you needed to do to break into the into the AFL ranks.

Torch: And what position where they playing you, Ben?

Ben Moore: A little bit of anything, on the ball and a little bit or up forward. I'm just a little fella but I could run around.

Richo: But you must have been doing what Wallsy

wanted because you were drafted in '95 and you broke through for your first game in your first season, which doesn't always happen.

Ben Moore: No, you're right. And you set yourself goals but when you set out in your first pre-season, you feel a long way off. So I was pretty pumped to be able to sort of play league footy within the first year. And then it was a couple of games there, a couple of games here for four years and then back to Adelaide.

Richo: Four years in Melbourne and you were let go. Was going back to Adelaide a natural thing to do?

Ben Moore: That's where all the family and friends and all that were. It was just an easy transition to come back home and get back into regular life.

Billy: How did they break it to you that your time at Richmond had come to a logical conclusion?

Ben Moore: It's hard to remember back then but it wasn't much because they had another coaching change where Danny Frawley stepped in and I think he moved on maybe 10 or 12 of us. There wasn't a lot of communication. It was just unfortunately a change of coach and he wanted some new blood.

Billy: And did you go home and skipper Glenelg straight away? Or did you work your way up to the captaincy?

Ben Moore: No, I put in about three or four years just playing for the [Glenelg] Tigers. And then I was lucky enough as the general progression, I got a bit older and a bit more experienced. And I was given the honour of skippering the club for a couple of years which was nice.

Covey: Being a Glenelg boy initially, had you barracked for Richmond in the VFL?

Ben Moore: No, I grew up here when the Crows made their introduction into the AFL.

Richo: And everyone knows that the Crows are really just a Glenelg front.

Ben Moore: It was early on in the piece.

Covey: For those people that can't recall Ben Moore playing his 24 games with the Tiges back between '96 and '99, you did describe yourself as a small player who played around the middle and forward a bit, and I note you wore the No. 28 jumper. Were you sort of like Jake King before Jake King came along?

Ben Moore: Yeah, just without the muscles and the push ups! And I think he would have racked up a few more games than me right now.

Covey: And talking about racking up games, given that you did go at No. 46 in the draft ahead of Brent Harvey at 47, do you marvel at the fact that he is still going around?

Ben Moore: He is a marvel, mate. I run around with my kids in the park and I can't walk the next day. And this guy's sort of, you know, pumping out some terrific footy at his age at AFL level. He's done very well for himself. There's not too many that can do what he's done.

Billy: And do you keep in contact with your old Richmond teammates?

Ben Moore: To be honest, not a lot. My best man at my wedding was Ross Funcke who used to play at Richmond and other than that you sort of drift apart and unfortunately it's just the natural progression when kids and life gets in the way.

Covey: And you're still down at Glenelg?

Ben Moore: Yeah, I moved away for a little while. I played a bit of country footy and coached out at the country and now I'm just back as an assistant coach in the mid-field just to help out the club that I love and owe a bit to.

Richo: We don't pay as much attention to the SANFL any more since the Crows and Port have come into the AFL but I'm assuming that Port Adelaide is still the team you want to beat the most?

Ben Moore: When you're Glenelg, your arch rivals are always Port Adelaide. They changed the name to Power from the Magpies but they're still black and white.

Richo: Yeah, well, we'll be watching Glenelg very closely for the rest of the year. And it's been tremendous talking with you this morning Ben. Thank you so much.

Ben Moore: No worries. Thanks for having me.

Richo: Ben Moore there, taken at pick No. 46 in the 1995 draft, one pick before Brent Harvey at 47.

The South Australians

TOM WARHURST

Tom Warhurst had a decade-long SANFL career with Norwood behind him when he was first picked in the inaugural Adelaide squad and then in the team for the Crows' debut AFL match. He played the next week, but his AFL career ended at two games and his SANFL days were over at the end of that 1991 season as well, curtailed by a serious knee injury.

Richo: Welcome to the Coodabeens, Tom Warhurst.

Tom Warhurst: Good afternoon lads, how are you?

Richo: How well do you remember that first game?

Tom Warhurst: Reasonably well, it was a quite a big occasion here in Adelaide at the time. And although I played 10 years of footy in the SANFL, and a couple of state games, it was a highlight.

Richo: Now when it all started, you were a Norwood player, do you remember who tapped you on the shoulder and said, Look, you want to join this new thing? Because everyone knew at the time that although they had a different jumper it was basically a Glenelg thing, wasn't it?

Tom Warhurst: It was a Glenelg thing and we hated Glenelg and still hate Glenelg and we didn't like Cornesy too much. And then, all of a sudden, you're thrown into the change room with Port players and guys that you hated and belted over the years, and it was all a bit awkward at the start.

Covey: So how did you cope with that?

Tom Warhurst: Although, you did find out that the guys in the other teams were quite reasonable lads, I don't think we ever learned to cope with it to be honest. Now they don't have that SANFL allegiance those young lads who play for the Crows, but in the early days, you never got over it. I still dislike the teammates from the other teams.

Torch: Tom, going into that game, Hawthorn was pretty much the best side in the comp at that stage. Did you give yourselves a chance to beat them?

Tom Warhurst: I probably didn't at the time. They had just won the night Premiership and they had all the stars, they had the Dunstalls and the Breretons and I hadn't played against Victoria in State footy so I had no real knowledge of what I was up against. But at quarter-time we certainly rated ourselves because we were a few goals up and we were on a bit of a roll and the crowd was just fantastic.

Champs: Tom my memory of the game was McDermott who was captain got crunched by a Dermie sandwich. I forget who else was in the sandwich. Maybe Dermie sandwiched him alone.

Tom Warhurst: Dermott cleaned him up after he got rid of it. I was standing Dermie at the time and I was about 15 metres away doing the weak thing calling for the handball and it ultimately cost me I think, because Cornesy and the guys didn't look kindly on the fact that I didn't remonstrate and go and put Dermie on his backside. So I think that was partly the reason why I was on my way shortly after.

Champs: The crowd got fired up with that one as you'd expect and it seemed to help things along for the Crows.

DERMIE
SANDWICH

Tom Warhurst: Exactly, Dermott was a fantastic player but he wasn't highly regarded in Adelaide for one reason or another. I can't remember what stage of the game it was, maybe the third quarter, but I think we were well on the way to winning by then.

Richo: Tom, you will get the amazing credit that you're a member of that inaugural Crows squad that played in that amazing game.

Tom Warhurst: Go ahead and say it, I'm a Trivial Pursuit question.

Richo: Little did you know at the time you were only going to play one more game, which was the following week, and never get back. Do you think you were just a victim of the Glenelg anti-Norwood feeling in the Crows at the time?

Tom Warhurst: The real reason is probably that Steven Kernahan kicked five the next week against me and unbeknown to people, about six weeks later, I had a knee reconstruction. So no, it was a combination of things. But Cornesy and I have a love-hate relationship so it probably didn't help that I was from the wrong side of town, in his eyes anyway.

Covey: That's a better trivia question, isn't it? Who did Stephen Kernahan kick five on?

Tom Warhurst: Well you'd probably come up with about 30 different people.

Covey: Another Glenelg bloke, Stephen Kernahan. Hey Tom, just backtracking to that very first game, when you had that fantastic win and then you went back to the rooms. I know, it was way back in 1991, but I'm trying to think how long this phenomenon has been going on. Did you stand in a circle and sing the club song? And if so, had you practiced it?

Tom Warhurst: I'm pretty confident that we didn't have a club song yet! In fact, it was only about six weeks prior to that we'd seen the jumper and we knew what we were going to be called. It was a ridiculous situation, to be honest.

Champs: Your club song was actually *here we go, here we go, Camry Crows.*

Tom Warhurst: There might have been a 'kick a Vic' somewhere in there too.

Covey: It's sad enough that you only got to play two games and then had a knee reco and never reappeared. But I'm even more saddened that you didn't get to sing the song Tommy!

Tom Warhurst: Well, exactly right. I'd much rather reflect on the years I had at Norwood. I see myself as a Norwood man rather than a Crow.

Covey: Let's do that. How many years did you have at Norwood?

Tom Warhurst: Ten years at Norwood, 248 games, so I'm much prouder of those facts.

Covey: Are you allowed to add the two Crows games to the 248 at Norwood and make 250 games of league footy?

Tom Warhurst: No, in fact they wouldn't give me league life membership because in fact I was 249 and league life membership was 250.

Billy: That's an outrage.

Champs: And Tom, your dad was a legend of SA footy.

Tom Warhurst: Yeah, he was he was a legend in a lot of sports. He actually played tennis for Australia and made the quarter-final of an Australian Open as well as being vice-captain at Norwood and losing a Magarey on a count-back and all sorts of things. So he was he was a talented all-rounder.

Champs: How many games for him?

Tom Warhurst: Well, he spent five years in the war so he only played 99 games. We have a history of ending up with one short.

Billy: Does he get life membership for being runner-up in the Magarey?

Tom Warhurst: No, he didn't. And no life membership for spending five years in the desert somewhere.

Covey: Has there ever been a family harder done by in football than the Warhurst family?

Tom Warhurst: You'll have to start an appeal!

Champs: My memory of your dad Tom was the sport panels. He was a media commentator.

Tom Warhurst: He was very popular on Channel 7 footy and as a commentator on radio 5KA. He's passed on now, Dad but I still have many people saying that they have fond memories of the old man.

Champs: He had the mo.

Tom Warhurst: He did have the mo, very dapper.

Richo: Tom you've told us that you see yourself as a Norwood player. Not really a Crows player. That in the modern game now what is it now, 18 years on, who do you barrack for?

Tom Warhurst: I don't follow an AFL team to be honest.

Richo: That's true South Australian values.

Tom Warhurst: I like watching a good AFL game of footy but I find there's very few games that I can watch the full 100 minutes of. I like watching Geelong and Hawthorn and Collingwood can play good footy but then it tails off a bit. I'm interested in the footy but I watched the first 15 or 20 minutes and then turn it off on most occasions. I'd rather watch the SANFL or amateur league it's the way the game was meant to be played.

Billy: That's true traditional values when Adelaide people did couldn't even name the VFL teams much less barrack for one of them.

Tom Warhurst: People might say it's old-timers talking but it's all too regimented and kicking backwards and all this kind of stuff.

Covey: And what about the move to get footy back to the Adelaide Oval? Have you got a view on that?

Tom Warhurst: I think it's fantastic, Footy Park is just too far away. It's a four or five-hour round trip, you might as well put it in Horsham or somewhere like that.

Covey: Well, as soon they start playing at the Adelaide Oval, I'm coming over and we'll go to the footy together Tom, it'll be a marvellous day. We can pop in to the Festival Theatre after the first 15 minutes!

Tom Warhurst: Sounds good.

Richo: Tom, thanks very much for joining us.

MALCOLM GREENSLADE

Malcolm Greenslade was a young school teacher whose life was turned upside down when his number was called in the national service draft in the middle of the Vietnam War. That he also happened to be one of the best footballers in the SANFL was a fact exploited by Richmond who played Malcolm while he was on basic training in Victoria. His VFL career totalled just the two highlight-filled games in 1971 before returning to Sturt, depriving Victorian football fans of seeing one of the era's great players on a regular basis. Malcolm joined the show on Anzac Day 2009 to reminisce.

Richo: Those of us who are old enough all remember one of the marks of the century, it's right up there in the top 10 marks ever out at Waverley in Round 3, 1971. It was taken by Malcolm Greenslade who was doing national service at the time. Malcolm joins us online now. Malcolm, welcome to the Coodabeens.

Malcolm Greenslade: Thanks very much.

Richo: Tell us about that time you were a highly rated player in the SANFL and all of a sudden your number came up in the draft.

Malcolm Greenslade: It was actually quite traumatic. When you're that age, you've actually just got your career established and I'd had a year at Unley High School teaching PE. I was deeply involved in a relationship, which I still am with my wife, and my world just seemed to sort of plummet a bit. And to try and appreciate the fact that you were going to be committed, literally to being ripped out of home, put in an environment that you actually wonder whether you could cope with, with maybe the possibility of going away overseas, for a 20-year-old was pretty heavy to handle.

Billy: Was the transition made any easier once you're actually in training, Malcolm?

Malcolm Greenslade: Well, you lost contact with those things that were comfortable around you at home. And the basic training we did at Pucka really got you into a vision that this was going to be your life for at least two years. As it transpired it was only for 18 months, but it changed your outlook. I think in some ways, I actually got quite bitter about the whole situation, I guess it was a very selfish outlook that I had adopted at that time.

Billy: You would have been serving with other young men who felt exactly the same, I'm sure.

Malcolm Greenslade: Well, I had my buddy there Michael Nunan and we actually both went in at the same time and as luck or good fortune would have it we actually served most of our time together until I came back here to Adelaide.

Covey: Was the entire 18 months at Puckapunyal, Malcolm?

Malcolm Greenslade: No, I did the 10-week basic training at Puckapunyal and then I got a posting to the Signal Corps where I went to Watsonia and served there and I actually did a driver's course at Broadmeadows. During that time, after I played for Richmond, I actually came back and played for Sturt on the weekends and got cleaned up out at Elizabeth and ended up in the Repat Hospital. And that meant that I spent my last eight months here in Adelaide and I actually worked out at Keswick as a teacher.

Covey: Just how far into your training was it when you were able to get released to go and play with Richmond?

Malcolm Greenslade: It was quite near the end of it almost near the parade that we had when we left and went to our core postings and I remember getting picked in, I think it must have been game two, and the army said no, you can't do that because we've got the parade and you've got to practice loading your rifle, polishing your boots, cleaning your brass and doing all that.

Billy: When you turned up at Richmond, were they welcoming or did they say 'Who are you mate?'

Malcolm Greenslade: No, there had been quite a lot of conversations. And it was with a number of clubs that were able to take advantage of this national service transition, where you moved from one state to another. And so there were about three or four certain reasons why I opted for Richmond.

Covey: Having played those couple of games for the Tigers, would you like to have ended up playing more VFL footy?

Malcolm Greenslade: Yes, I can say that now and critically yes I would have, but at the time you've got to put it all into perspective that here was a little kid who liked being at home and had his girlfriend at home, had the comfortable things at home and here was an option to come back to Adelaide every weekend, catch the plane back Sunday night and then go about your business in your khaki uniform during the week. And so, yes, I would have loved now to see whether I really would have been able to establish myself in that competition but, at the time, the opportunity to just come home totally overrode that.

Richo: Malcolm, you played the two games for Richmond, what were your goal-kicking totals?

Malcolm Greenslade: I kicked one goal at Waverley against St

Kilda and I kicked six against South Melbourne at the Lakeside Oval.

Richo: And which of those games did Michael Nunan play with you?

Malcolm Greenslade: Mick played with me in the one against South Melbourne. It was quite interesting that game because John Murphy, former vice-captain of the Sturt footy club, was playing for South Melbourne at that time.

Torch: Of course, one of your teammates at that time was Royce Hart at Richmond and he had the amazing stat that he played in two Grand Finals in a week. And he didn't have to change his jumper because he was playing for Glenelg is that right?

Malcolm Greenslade: That was a memorable one when Terry Short cleaned him up.

Richo: In the first two minutes.

Covey: Malcolm, we talked about those couple of games you did play and there is that famous photograph of you leaping high to mark out at Waverley. And there's people sitting on the concrete terraces because they hadn't installed the seats. Can you recall the mark and how did you get up so high?

Malcolm Greenslade: Well, thanks to Roger Dean for getting up so high but it was actually my very first kick in VFL footy, which made it a bit more special. And I guess it was just one of those things that when you're playing footy and you love the game and you think you're Superman you just go for it.

Richo: So that was your first touch and it is still regarded as one of the marks of the century the whole footy world was alive with it and remarkably, it was captured in one of the great footy photographs of all time, which was on the front page of every paper the next day.

Malcolm Greenslade: I believe that's right, but to me it was just a mark and until we actually looked at it that night, it was just the mark and part of the game. I do remember that the kick actually did result in a goal because it went straight to Royce Hart which was something that I'm glad happened.

Billy: Was Roger dirty on you that you kneed him in the back of the scone, Malcolm?

Malcolm Greenslade: Well I did have a look at the photo and the leg's pretty well up around his neck.

Covey: You played at Waverley and you played down at the Lake Oval, did you also play on the MCG for South Australia?

Malcolm Greenslade: Yes, I did.

Covey: And you went alright that day didn't you?

Malcolm Greenslade: I kicked six goals on that day. We actually were unfortunate not to win that game, we just lost it by not a big margin and that was memorable, it was truly a highlight of football for me in particular at that time where life was a bit confused.

Covey: Interestingly I think you kicked something like the first five of those six goals on John Scarlett another ex-serviceman before they swung Vinnie Waite onto you?

Malcolm Greenslade: No, I think I ended up with Scarlett all day. Waite was the one that headbutted me though and put me out.

Covey: And Malcolm, what about today on Anzac Day, do you go to Anzac Day dawn services or observances?

Malcolm Greenslade: I have been to an Anzac day service here in Adelaide, in fact, in 1995 I had a backpack on the back and went to Europe for four months, I was 45 so I had a bit of a head on me that I could actually think rationally. I went to

Gallipoli and thoroughly enjoyed the total experience there just by myself and then later I toured the battlefields up in Belgium and France. I have a bit of a feeling more so now than at the time when I actually wore the uniform.

Billy: It would have made national service a bit more resonant for you.

Malcolm Greenslade: Much more significant and I have more of a feeling for those people that actually endured the terrible nature of what war was really about.

Billy: What's Micky Nunan up to now?

Malcolm Greenslade: Michael's got himself ensconced up around the hills area here and he works with horses. Michael has a business with heart rate monitors, a very successful business and he has been able to transfer that from the human body to take on the horses and use as a training aid. It's been a very, very successful business for him, I was very fortunate to catch up with him only a couple weeks ago when he came to my son's wedding, we had a fantastic chat.

Covey: And Malcolm what about from the footy side of things are you still involved or take interest?

Malcolm Greenslade: Yes, I am. I've actually been an assistant coach for the state Under 16s here in South Australia and we're taking part in the national championships for that age group in Sydney in early July. It's a great opportunity to work with and just see the transition of some of our youth here who have committed themselves to playing football. As a matter of fact after this call gets hung up I'm off to Prospect to have a look at some of them play in what we've got here is teeming rain.

Covey: Well there's only one thing you've got to show them as you're coaching them Malcolm, just show them the photo of the mark over Roger Dean and that's how it's done.

Richo: And Malcolm of course, you're too modest to mention it yourself, but South Australian schoolboy football is recognised every year with the Malcolm Greenslade Medal.

Malcolm Greenslade: Yes, there is a medal named after me for the Year 8/9 knockout competition for secondary school sport. I must admit I did actually say to them that it's got a five-year life because I believe sometimes these things have other people who are more deserving who can come in and perhaps take it. But I'm very proud of that.

Covey: Malcolm, it's been great to have you, as blokes who grew up in that era of football. We've been doing this show for a long time and it has been one of the most enjoyable 10 minutes of chatting to someone on the program. It's been great. Malcolm.

Malcolm Greenslade: Thank you very much. I really appreciate it, that's very generous of you.

Richo: Malcolm, thanks so much for joining us. And I hope you have a terrific day watching the footy with the juniors at Prospect today and send some of that rain over the border please.

Malcolm Greenslade: I'm sure it's coming. And when it comes, it's going to dump a lot.

Richo: Looking forward to it. Malcolm Greenslade, sensational player of the '70s in the SANFL and of course famously played those two games for Richmond while he was doing national service.

Covey: And he played just enough games for a number of commentators to put an S on the on the end of Greenslade(s)!

JOHN NOACK

Talented young Sturt ruckman John Noack came to Geelong for one year as part of his studies. A young man needs an outlet from the classroom and John found his way to Kardinia Park, on to the Cats' senior list and into the team for one game against North Melbourne on 1 July 1967.

Richo: Good to have you with us at the MCG this morning, John.

John Noack: I'm delighted to be here, thank you.

Covey: This is a rare treat for Billy and me because we were there when you played your one game, John.

John Noack: Sorry, I can't remember seeing you in the crowd.

Billy Baxter: Oh, we saw you. We were very impressed, too.

Covey: Well, you played in an era when the great Polly Farmer was still playing in 1967.

John Noack: Not the great, the greatest player in that era.

Billy Baxter: And some people say that John carried Polly Farmer.

Covey: And he did! Tell us the story about carrying Polly Farmer, John.

John Noack: Well, Peter Pianto gave us a routine to go across the Kardinia Park oval on each other's shoulders and I jumped on Polly's shoulders and went across but then, at the other side, we had to swap and so I had to carry Polly from one side to the other and I can certainly indicate that he wasn't just a great player, but he was also a pretty heavy player.

Richo: Now, John, you played senior footy in the SANFL before coming across?

John Noack: Yes, down in South Australia I was playing for Sturt. I played some games but we had Doc Clarkson who was a very good ruckman and it was very hard to get a regular spot at Sturt. And I was young and fairly light. I was only 13 stone. I remember playing against Norwood and Glenelg, but otherwise it was with the reserves, which I thoroughly enjoyed.

Champs: And was Jack Oatey still the coach?

John Noack: Yes, Jack was still the coach and an excellent coach. He actually had a technique where he got Clarkson to ruck from the same side as the opposing ruckman. It was a negating sort of style and that became his standard way of doing it.

Richo: So, who from Geelong spotted you and got you over, John?

John Noack: I really don't know, someone must have heard I was coming over and then they said would you come down for a training run.

Richo: Oh, you were coming over anyway?

John Noack: I was coming over for the year as part of my occupation training for a year of practical work. And so I went on the pre-season training run with 100 players who were trying to get on the squad of 36 or so. I ran like the dickens up the sand hills, along the beach and over fences at Dr. Threlfall's property down near the beach. And we had a very long cross country run where I came in third and Doug Wade, I think, came in last.

Billy: There's some talk that Doug is just finishing now! So, you made it onto the list obviously.

John Noack: Oh yes, I got onto the 36 list, which meant that I had a regular spot in the reserves and was available if I was needed in the seniors but, of course, Polly Farmer and John Newman were pretty good ruckmen. It was a bit hard to get a regular spot in the seniors but I was rucking in the reserves with Ian Hampshire.

Covey: You mentioned Doug Wade during that training, didn't you have an incident where you clashed with Doug Wade in a practice match?

John Noack: Yes. Somehow or other, he ran into my chin. And I just kept playing but he got carted off the ground. And one of the newspapers saw that was rather strange that he had to go off the ground and I kept playing.

Covey: Not a good thing for a young player who is trying to make his way to go injuring the great Doug Wade and having him sent off the ground, John.

John Noack: Yes, I can't recall, but I really think it was his fault. He must have run into me.

Billy Baxter: It got better than that, John said I've taken Wadey out, I'm going to have a go at that goal post now and you ran full pelt into a goal post.

John Noack: That's right and they say the goal posts really bend over but the point was I hit it side on and it was the whole side of my body that hit the goal post and I didn't feel a thing you see.

Richo: Well, it must have impressed Peter Pianto and the selectors because you were called up for Round 11 at home,

Kardinia Park, for your first game in the ones for the Cats. Tell us about how that came about John.

John Noack: Well, they wanted to try out some new players. And we'd been playing hard in the reserves and we did get ourselves in the finals at the end. They thought John Scarlett should be given a go, I should be given a go and Brown the rover, too. And Hughie Strahan was another one. We were all given a go and we were very pleased but the next week the main ruckmen were back in business again and I was back in the reserves. But being in the reserves, you can enjoy football as much as anywhere else. So, I've always enjoyed my football, even though I'm a One Game Wonder.

Covey: Who were you opposed to that day against North Melbourne?

John Noack: Peter Pianto told me to negate their ruckman Barry Goodingham who was taller than I was. But obviously I tried to do the best I could and Peter Pianto was happy that I had succeeded in keeping him down as much as possible.

Richo: But at the time you must've thought, well, this is alright, I'll get another game here. How long did you stay on at Geelong?

John Noack: Well, I was there just for the one year. I then went back to Adelaide and so I thought it's very good of Geelong to actually put me on the 36 for the year.

Richo: And how about the finals campaign? You were playing for the Geelong reserves through the finals?

John Noack: Yes, yes. I just forget how far we got but we didn't make the Grand Final.

Torch: One of the more bizarre things that happened in 1967, which you might remember, was the fact that Denis Marshall because he lived in Melbourne...

Covey: Oh, here we go, he trained at South Melbourne.

Torch: He trained at South Melbourne, on Tuesday nights, then he trained at Geelong on a Thursday night.

John Noack: Yes, and we heard all about that. Apparently, when Geelong were playing South, the South team were discussing how they could floor Marshall and get him out of the way. Someone in Geelong was listening into the talk and they came into our rooms and said, 'I got a message for Marshall, just watch out'.

Champs: Torchy was on the bench for South when John made his debut for Geelong that round.

Torch: That's right, sitting next to Bobby Mallett who ended up at Port Melbourne.

Covey: John, when you did go back to South Australia the next year 1968, you played for the delightfully named Freeling Redlegs in the Barossa and Light Football Association. Greg Champion is from South Australia. Greg, Freeling?

Champs: Freeling is where they've since been shooting McLeod's Daughters, John. It is a beautiful little village near Kapunda, just stuck there in the paddocks.

John Noack: Just north of the Barossa Valley. They'd heard that I was coming back to South Australia and they were very keen to have me up in the Barossa and Light and I thought, well, I'd probably get more reliable games up there than trying to fight against Clarkson at Sturt and so I had an excellent year. And I was very pleased at the end of the year that they kept calling me to dinners and they gave me a few medals at the end of it so that made the year very enjoyable.

Covey: People go on about how Tony Liberatore won all these

medals, but he won them in different years. You won three in one year.

John Noack: Well, there was the Freeling club one, and then there was the association one and then the umpires called me into a dinner for the South Australian umpiring, across all the leagues in South Australia, and I ended up winning their medal. I probably did better than if I'd played for Sturt.

Covey: When you go to a Barossa and Light Football Association match, instead of getting a couple of cans at the beer stall, do they just have, you know, a cheeky Chardonnay on sale?

John Noack: No comment!

Richo: John, have you maintained your allegiance to the Cats?

John Noack: Oh, yes, yes. And I have been able to attend some very impressive functions. The Cats' Tales was a magnificent night going back through all the eras.

Covey: And are you going in a couple of weeks' time to the big 150th celebration?

John Noack: Oh, yes, I won't miss out on that.

Richo: John, you played in an era where you found it very hard to force your way into the Geelong side because there wasn't one but there were two outstanding ruckmen and then another two very good ones in the reserves. And yet we've got Geelong this season, sort of getting by without really a big name recognised ruckman at all, what's your view on ruckwork in modern footy?

John Noack: Well, mostly it hasn't changed but Polly, of course, developed the technique of scooping the ball and handpassing it on. It was very much about his body work, not relying on the big knock. I really think that if the ruckmen can develop that sort of thing where they are working very closely with their rovers that's better than just a knock that may go anywhere. But I can't really comment on today's situation. It's a bit hard.

Richo: It's light years away.

Covey: John was first at the ground this morning and he's got his Cats scarf on, too, which is fantastic to see. And do you take a particular interest in the player wearing No. 9, which you donned for your one game?

John Noack: I have been, yes. Kelly and Turner before him and, of course, I had it after John Devine so it's a bit of interest.

Richo: It's got a good story, the No. 9, and thank you John Noack for sharing your story with us this morning.

Covey: And Richo, there can't be too many people in football who can boast that they played for Sturt and Geelong as well as the beautiful Freeling and, not to forget, Rainbow up in the Hopetoun league.

John Noack: That's right. We actually won the Grand Final there in 1970. So that's one Grand Final for me.

Richo: Well, there's plenty of people who haven't got one. John, thanks very much for joining us and enjoy the rest of the day here at the MCG.

John Noack: Thank you very much.

JOHN KLUG

John Klug was a Tasmanian in South Australia playing for Woodville when he was invited to train with the new Adelaide Crows in 1990. He became a mainstay in their first season in the AFL, but a mixture of injury and form limited his career to just 26 senior games over two years. He has one claim to fame though, he had the first possession ever recorded by an Adelaide Crows player in the AFL. It was a handball, in that famous first win against Hawthorn at Football Park and that was the reason we tracked John down in 2013.

Richo: The legendary John Klug joins us on the line now, welcome to the Coodabeens.

John Klug: Thanks a lot.

Covey: And that handball was back in 1991, so Johnny, we imagine for 22 years you've just been living off it?

John Klug: I organise sportsman's nights, but they don't have a lot of attendees.

Champs: Klugie, I think you were from Tassie weren't you?

John Klug: Yes I was, and I'm back there now at a place called Lauderdale, about 20km south of Hobart.

Champs: Are you involved in footy?

John Klug: I'm assistant coach at the Lauderdale footy club. Mitch Robinson is our most famous export.

Richo: John, tell us about the period where the Crows were forming up and who got in touch with you to get you to Adelaide.

John Klug: I played for Woodville Warriors and I think I was the 97th guy picked in the squad; a bloke named Wayne Weidemann was the 98th. And we trained through the pre-season in the hope that we would actually get picked. They had about 10 guys from the AFL—guys like McGuinness, Danny Hughes, Mark Mickan, established players, but the rest of us were just scrubbers from the local league.

Billy: John, this segment is about firsts and you got the first possession in the Crows history, which was a handball. Can you talk us through it?

John Klug: I actually can't remember it! It was a long time ago. I do remember that the night itself was a fantastic night, obviously we won, which was pretty rare in those days. I worked at Westpac till about three o'clock, then I carried the bag across and then all of a sudden we're playing in front of 40,000 people. The first possession I can't remember but I didn't have too many more after that.

Covey: You were clearly in at the first bounce.

John Klug: No, I was at centre half-forward so it must have just dribbled forward. I think big Romano Negri, a fellow Tasmanian, got the tap down and I don't know what happened, I wouldn't have had it for too long because I would have got caught!

Torch: In that game, you were playing against the Premiers too.

John Klug: They had won the night Premiership a week before and I remember watching it on television thinking oh my god, what have I got myself in for, but I think we just had an adrenaline burst and ended up winning by around 12 or 14 goals.

Covey: 24.11.155 to Hawthorn 9.15.69. Hawthorn went on to win the Premiership that year, Collingwood were the Premiers in 1990.

Champs: Klugie, I never knew that Romano Negri was from Tassie too.

John Klug: Romy and I were in that first game together and we caught up a couple of years ago with the 20th anniversary. He played about four or five games and we were just very lucky to be there at the right time and it was just a brilliant time. I was very lucky to get a few AFL games in before they got a reasonable side.

Billy: We have the stats in front of us from the particular game, Johnny, and you're underselling yourself. You might not remember your first handball, but of the 24 goals that Adelaide amassed they've got you down here for four. Can you remember any of the goals?

John Klug: Just a couple of little snaps off the pack. No, not really, again, it was just a blur the whole experience but it was more about the crowd and the fact that we won and that was huge. I remember a couple of weeks before, we played Essendon in a practice match and I was with Nigel Smart who became a legend. We drove to the game and we called in at Hungry Jack's for a Whopper. And we were in my '74 Corolla and I said, gee, the traffic's a bit thick Nige, and there were about 40,000 people coming to a practice match! So I suppose from then we realised we were part of something and the Crows were always going to be successful and pretty huge.

Richo: John, you were a part of it but we were sitting back

I HAD
TO COME
STRAIGHT
FROM WORK
10
7

here watching it saying, 'Who's this "Plug" bloke? Why didn't we get him?' And all these players no one had seen and no one had heard of and I don't think anyone had seen a haircut or a moustache as neat and tidy as David Marshall's.

John Klug: Now he was a well-groomed man, and still is! He looked exactly the same when I saw him last year.

Covey: Looking at the stats from that match, David Marshall was making his debut at 30 years of age.

John Klug: I was 25, we had Grantley Fielke who was a really good footballer, he was about the same. I would have loved to see McDermott go a few years earlier because he would have been an absolute superstar. We had Jars too—Andrew Jarman.

Champs: Can we just go back for a minute, did you say you carried your bag across from Westpac?

John Klug: In those days we weren't paid a lot and had to work in real jobs but they did allow me to knock off at three o'clock which was nice of them. I worked in the bank at Westlakes Shopping Centre across from the ground. I'm assuming it still exists.

Champs: It does. And you walked across in your Westpac shirt with your kitbag at 3pm after a day's work, amazing.

Covey: Did you get mobbed in the car park before the game?

John Klug: I had a pen but no one came up to me!

Billy: Did you ask for No. 20 John?

John Klug: I was given it but I was very proud this year that a kid from Lauderdale named Sam Siggins got the jumper so hopefully, he'll get more games than I did.

Champs: In those early days, we had Darren Smith at times as a key forward, we had Scotty Hodges, but the times that John

Klug occupied the spot, as a Crow fan I thought this guy gives us something. How did you feel about your place in the team?

John Klug: I wasn't a great player and once Adelaide started to get better players in, they shoved us out. I had knee injuries which curtailed my career a little bit in the end. But at the end of the day, I was just very pleased to have been part of it and it was nice to be part of something special.

Richo: John, tell us about Cornesy.

John Klug: Eccentric is the best word to describe Graham! But he did a fantastic job when you look back. They should have made the Grand Final in their third year. He was mad about football, while probably a lot of us loved footy but we didn't live it which Graham struggled with, but he was a coach before his time. There were a few guys that could have been drafted but weren't, like Smarty and Bickley, who got into the system under Graham and developed into sensational footballers.

Champs: And John, you didn't stick around in Adelaide after the Crows?

John Klug: No, I got the chop after the third year, '93 and came back to Tassie.

Richo: You've obviously still got a real soft spot for the Crowies though, are they your team?

John Klug: Yes, they are. It's hard not to when you're part of the inauguration of the club.

Covey: And when you were playing for Woodville, before you went to the Crowies, did you play on the Adelaide Oval?

John Klug: I did. South Adelaide and Sturt played their home games at the Adelaide Oval. It's probably my favourite oval in Australia.

Covey: What's it going to be like when they get footy back there soon?

John Klug: It's a ground that has atmosphere even when nobody is there. North Hobart in Tassie is a bit the same and obviously the MCG is not too bad. It will be a great move, because the crowds have dropped in South Australia over the last couple years.

Covey: And boys working in the bank in North Terrace won't have far to walk down to the ground!

Richo: John, thank you so much.

John Klug: Great talking to you this morning.

Richo: John Klug, the man who got the very first stat for the Crows in their first game in the league.

straight away. I've never experienced this before but they just dropped their bundle straight away and we went on and won. But I think that was the big thing that I noticed because I'd never seen it before. I'd been in the '70s with North—a very successful side. But never did I feel that the opposition gave up.

Champs: Port just had them spooked.

Mark Dawson: One of the myths was that when the opposition bus came past the Cheltenham cemetery in the suburb next to Port Adelaide, that's where everything changed. It seemed like that when you were playing for them as well, I can tell you.

Billy: In making the switch Mark, did you actually meet Russell Ebert?

Mark Dawson: Yes, he used to come back to Adelaide from time to time and I got to know him and we had a few beers and it was strange because we were at each other's footy clubs by then but I was always a North person and Russell was always a Port person. So I think for the two of us, we were we were always going to be favourites of the clubs that we left so Russell was always going to go back to Port Adelaide and Ron told me that I'll just go over there and win a Magarey Medal and then come back to North and get paid twice as much money. But that didn't happen! I got to know Russ reasonably well, he was a superstar, though I'm not sure North used him to his best advantage by playing him in the back pocket. He was a very big centreman and strong and I think he won four Magareys and ran second a few times. So that's how good he was, he was an absolute standout superstar.

Covey: Did you go better at Port than Russell went at North? You can wrap yourself up Mark!

Mark Dawson: No, we won flags in '79, '80 and '81, I played in '79, did my knee and my shoulder and tried to get fit again and come back in '80. I played one game and then played the second game and walked off at quarter-time and never played again. That was the end of my career because I'd just worn through the bone in my knee and the articular cartilage and that was the end of it. But I certainly know that I brought a lot of things to the table at Port Adelaide that we did at North and what I'd been taught by Barass. There was a point in time one day when we weren't winning games that we should have been winning and Jack basically said do whatever you like and we're Port Adelaide so we should win. And I started to get a bit frustrated because there was no discipline in the place. And even though when I was at North I was always trying to get out of everything, I finished up one day saying to Jack [John Cahill], you sit down there and be quiet while I address the boys. Now imagine doing that to Barass!

Covey: Of course you came back to North and you ended up on the board. And popular legend has it that you actually own the club. You were a shareholder, weren't you, Mark?

Mark Dawson: Yes, I was. When I came back to North I ran for Barry Cable for a couple of years. And then at a pre-season dinner I was a little bit outspoken and said something to Ron Joseph and Bob Ansett. And Ron said, 'You're such a smartarse, why don't you come on the board and put into practice what you're saying.' Albert Mantello was going to join the AFL Commission so they wanted me to take his place on the board. So that's basically how it happened. One of the things we quickly found out was that the club was bankrupt. Bob was bankrolling it through Tricontinental and the auditors found that this stream of money that was being paid for by Budget Rent-a-Car was going to fund North and then that got turned off very quickly. Then we had to make some pretty quick decisions. And I went out one night with Ron Joseph and said, come with me, we'll go and see some people and we knocked on people's doors. And I think I got home about two o'clock in the morning and we'd raised $2.1 million.

Richo: And, Mark, it's wonderful hearing you tell that story, because it's not just North supporters who are eternally grateful to you who pretty much saved North Melbourne, but everyone in footy, it just wouldn't be the same if North weren't in it. And it was a very close-run thing.

Mark Dawson: It was. I can remember going to talk to one guy and he asked how much did we need and I said, 'We're going to sell 10 shares for $300,000 each'. And he said, 'What do you get for that?' And I said, 'You get a seat on the board'. He said, 'But I want a say', so I said, 'Yeah, of course you're going to get a say'. This is a true story, he actually went for his bag, in his office, to get the $300,000 out of the bag. And I said 'No, no, no, we don't need it now!' And in the end, we got $600,000 off him!

Torch: And did he get a say?

Mark Dawson: No.

Billy: That is fantastic!

Mark Dawson: We eventually fell out over it because he wanted to know why he wasn't getting a say and I said, 'You just go and raise some sponsorship, don't worry about the team, you leave that to us'. It's funny when people get on boards, they always end up wanting to gravitate towards the team.

Richo: Mark those are just amazing stories. Thanks so much for sharing that with us.

Mark Dawson: Thanks guys.

Covey: Andy's on the phone out there, I think it's one of the producers of *Four Corners* on the line. They want to re-enact the $300,000 out of the bag in the office that night!

MICHAEL WRIGHT

When we spoke to Michael Wright in 2016, it was the second time we'd had him on the show. His first appearance was in 2010 as part of our 'Oh Brother' segment—Michael being the brother of Swans stalwart Stevie Wright. This time, it was due to the part he played in the complicated trade necessary to get SANFL star Peter Jonas to North Melbourne. The rest of the deal? North's Maurice Boyse was traded to South Melbourne and Michael left the VFL altogether, for Jonas' old SANFL club, Central Districts.

Richo: The other side of the Peter Jonas deal, Michael Wright, joins us on line right now. Welcome to the Coodabeens, Michael.

Michael Wright: Gentlemen, how are we?

Billy: Tell us about that deal Michael.

Michael Wright: What happened was I wanted to come to South Australia. I wasn't happy at South Melbourne because I didn't get on that well with our mate Stewy, so I decided to move over just after the 1980 Grand Final, which South and Geelong played in the reserves. I came over in the off season and I wanted to stay. Peter wanted to go to North to try his luck at VFL football but poor old Maurice had no idea what was happening. I believe on the Tuesday night once the clearances had all gone through, he was told that he was going to play at South Melbourne. He didn't want to go but at the end of the day he was forced into going I believe.

Covey: But you were happy with your end of the deal?

Michael Wright: At the time I was very happy because the money was quite good. Back in the '70s and '80s playing VFL football you virtually got nothing, you were working. The money that Centrals offered me was twice what I was getting playing VFL football and to play half the number of games so it was quite good.

Champs: And did you like the actual Central Districts club?

Michael Wright: I loved it. They were brilliant, a little bit like Geelong, as in it was out of town. Everybody knew you, people were right behind you, it might have been the poor end of town, but it was great fun.

Covey: Were Cold Chisel still in town at that stage?

Michael Wright: Good question. I believe they were but we never came across them.

Richo: And at the time we never saw this coming but two years later we had South Melbourne going to Sydney. There were you obviously very comfortable enjoying yourself over in Adelaide playing for Central Districts. But a lot of your former teammates were getting to go to Lady Fairfax's garden party.

Michael Wright: Exactly! But I almost got back. South Melbourne asked if I would come back and I said yes, I'd love to come back. Then once the decision was made to go to Sydney, Ricky Quade become coach and Greg Miller came over and we were just about putting pen to paper for me to go back to the Swans and in the last game of the '82 season for Centrals, I did a knee.

Billy: And that's footy isn't it? So that that last game knee injury it was between you having all the luxury and the glamour of Sydney lifestyle, and staying at Central Districts.

Michael Wright: Exactly right.

Covey: Did you ever cross paths with or meet Peter Jonas?

Michael Wright: Only when Peter came back to Centrals, if North Melbourne had a bye or a week off. A lot of his family was still involved in the football club, so we used to catch up a little bit and have a few drinks like everybody else used to do back then.

Torch: Now your junior footy would have been played at Oakleigh Districts, and a multitude of players who came out of Oakleigh Districts at that time ended up playing League footy. Why were they so successful?

Michael Wright: I think back in the day, the Federal league was very tough. You had the VFL, then you had the VFA, and Federal league was probably the next level down. A lot of older VFL footballers came into that league and when you were a kid they showed you how to play at the top level. So it became part and parcel, you knew that those guys were right behind you and that they would teach you how to do it. And I think at the time, a lot of scouts looked at you. And of course, you were zoned to an area, it wasn't like it is today.

Covey: You're still in South Australia, Michael. Where exactly do you live?

Michael Wright: We just moved to Gawler in the last 12 months. But we were up in the Riverland for about 20-odd years before that and loved it up there.

Champs: Gawler just proves that if you go far enough from Central Districts, you'll come back into a classy place again.

Torch: And which way do your AFL allegiances fall nowadays Michael?

Michael Wright: Still Sydney. When your brother was playing up there you've got to follow your brother.

Billy: So you're still a Blood.

Michael Wright: Still a Blood.

Richo: Great talking to you this morning, Michael. Thank you so much.

LEIGH CARLSON

When Magpie Leigh Carlson celebrated a win against North at Arden Street in May 1981, nobody could have expected that by the next Saturday he'd be a Lion. But this was the early '80s, the heyday of players swapping clubs, and Collingwood was desperate to get Fitzroy's Warwick Irwin. So instead of playing for Collingwood, Carlson crossed Smith Street to join the club he supported as a kid. He wasn't too happy about it though, as he told us in 2014.

Richo: Welcome to the Coodabeens.

Leigh Carlson: Good morning.

Richo: Tell us about how that whole deal unfolded.

Leigh Carlson: It was a disappointing time for me because I was quite entrenched at Collingwood. You'll remember that we played night games out at Waverley midweek, and the particular week in question we had a whole lot of rain, in fact, the game was washed out, it was called off on the Tuesday night. So we're at training Tuesday night instead and afterwards I got home and I was actually trying to fix a retaining wall that Tony Shaw had put up because soon after he put it up it had fallen down. I was out in the rain when the phone rings and my wife Kerry came out and said it's Fitzroy on the phone. and I thought what the bloody hell are they ringing me for? I went in and spoke to Arthur Wilson and I think as politely as I could hung up in his ear because I didn't want to know anything about it. I didn't know what was going on. I wondered why the hell they were ringing me and then George Coates rang about a half hour later and he said look Fitzroy have negotiated to change Warwick Irwin for yourself and Des Herbert and a young guy named Matt McClelland. And we've picked you to play on the wing against Footscray on the weekend.

Champs: How could they do that?

Leigh Carlson: My thoughts exactly. I said, 'I was picked on the wing at Collingwood last week, I was picked to play Tuesday night for Collingwood and I was hoping to be picked for Collingwood on Saturday, so I don't know what you're talking about'. And they said, 'Well, you better contact your club'. I rang the club and spoke to John Hickey [president] and it was quite late in the evening by that stage and John said they'd been talking to Fitzroy and that I had better speak to Tommy. So I rang Tommy and he rang back the next morning and he just said, 'We're really desperate to get Warwick Irwin, we think he's one of the 10 best players in the competition and we think we need him. You don't have to go but let me tell you he'll be playing in your spot so you make up your own mind'. I didn't think I really had much of a choice.

Billy: When do you reckon they would have told you?

Leigh Carlson: It would have been nice to have been informed before then.

Billy: So when did you meet your new teammates? And how long did you have to acquaint yourself with their style of play?

Leigh Carlson: I met them on Thursday and Robert Walls was coach and his theory was very different to Tom's. We trained for two hours every night with Tom, while with Wallsy we were on and off the track in half an hour. I said we only did the warm up, what's going on, so I'd only met them for half an hour. I'd been absolutely petrified playing against Ron Alexander for years. He used to punch me and hurt me, and the person I had the locker next to was Ron Alexander! I was frightened to say or do anything!

Torch: Where was Fitzroy's home ground at that time?

Leigh Carlson: That was at the Junction.

Richo: And while this whole change happened against your will and almost without your knowledge, you did step into what became a really exciting era at Fitzroy.

Leigh Carlson: It was. We had a great period through there. I think Wallsy was very much ahead of his time and he had a couple of really good people around him. I knew Chris Jones and Tony Knight were there as his fitness assistants and they were just outstanding in preparing us well. I knew Chris had a lot to do with basketball growing up and he was the one who started to talk to Wallsy about the huddle at centre half-back. But we were a good side.

Champs: Well Leigh, you've had a week of mixed emotions. How did it feel running out in a different jumper? And did you enjoy the game?

Leigh Carlson: I must admit, I was very lucky. Even arriving in those circumstances, the Fitzroy people welcomed me. They were just beautiful and really kind and gentle and I didn't get through the whole game, the week caught up with me. I think I was off by about 10 minutes into the last quarter with cramp.

Billy: And how long was it in that season before you met Collingwood in a match?

Leigh Carlson: It was late in the year and I have a feeling I kicked a late goal, I think not to win the game but to make it a certainty. It's fair to say I loved the Collingwood supporters, but I'm not sure they loved me on my return, they were pretty typical of the stories that I'd heard but had never seen.

Richo: Leigh, I tend to associate your career with Waverley a lot. I don't know why. You mentioned that that was back in the day when there was a midweek game on the Tuesday night and in my mind's eye whether it was in a Collingwood jumper or a Fitzroy jumper, it was always Carlson with the ball out at Waverley.

Leigh Carlson: I do cop quite a bit of ribbing about this. I think Lou Richards was the culprit, he nicknamed me The Night Owl which I wore for the rest of my playing career.

Billy: And how did Dessie Herbert and young Matt McClelland go at Fitzroy, Leigh?

Leigh Carlson: Dessie was quite a good player, I think we were probably both there for about three or four years after that. He probably played about 40 or 50 games. And Matt McClelland didn't go on and play senior footy.

Torch: During your time at Fitzroy, did you ever get a matchup on Warwick Irwin when you played Collingwood?

Leigh Carlson: Yes. In fact in a final where Collingwood beat us by a point or something after Ross Brewer kicked a goal over his head, I played on Warwick all of that game.

Billy: Who do you think got the best deal? Fitzroy or Collingwood.

Leigh Carlson: I'd like to think Fitzroy did but I'll leave others to decide that.

Torch: There was a difference in your ages wasn't there? Warwick I think was 29 and you were 21 so you had a few more years of football in front of you.

Leigh Carlson: Warwick in fact came back and played at Fitzroy after Collingwood. I think he was only there for a short period and he came back and played at Fitzroy.

Richo: Now Leigh, did you play all your junior footy in Preston?

Leigh Carlson: I did. Yes. I played at Regent and then as a 16-year-old I went and played at Preston.

Richo: And so traditionally Preston was either going to be Collingwood or Fitzroy in terms of people's allegiances, which were you Leigh?

Leigh Carlson: My dad was a sort of a Collingwood supporter, I think, originally and mum was a staunch Fitzroy supporter.

Torch: It was dependent on which side of High Street you lived on wasn't it?

Leigh Carlson: I think so. We were in what was called the little Chicago commission housing area. And I think it was mainly Collingwood there, but I barracked for Fitzroy, I was a mummy's boy and followed my mum.

Billy: And what was your relationship with Tommy like, thereafter?

Leigh Carlson: Look, Tom was just a wonderful man. I was really hurt by it but you know, back in those days we had after matches and both teams would go and have a feed and a cool drink and so forth. And every time I went in, Tommy was the first person to come up and speak to me when we're playing against Collingwood or Geelong, and he'd always ask after my wife Kerry and use her name. And about five years ago, I was sitting at a rugby game at Olympic Park watching Melbourne Storm, and he came up and sat next to me. So it was wonderful to catch up with him.

Richo: Now, Leigh, nowadays, when the ball's bounced and Collingwood are playing the Lions, which way do you lean?

Leigh Carlson: Do you want my truthful answer?

Richo: We want the answer that is in your best interest.

Leigh Carlson: Alright, I barrack for Storm.

Torch: So do you catch up with some of the past players from both sides?

Leigh Carlson: I see Pete Francis. Pete and I got to Fitzroy within about a month of each other. And we've maintained a family friendship all those years and still catch up and I'm godfather to one of his boys, Scotty and we see his family. And Neville Taylor, a little back pocket man who was tough as nails at Fitzroy. I don't see too many others. I see Shawry around the traps occasionally, we live not far from each other.

Richo: Just don't get him to do any more work in the garden.

Leigh Carlson: I haven't.

Richo: Leigh it's been wonderful talking to you this morning and revisiting what was a golden era of football in the early '80s. And your style of play was part of what lit it up. It's been terrific talking to you.

Leigh Carlson: Thank you very much. Have a good day.

Richo: Thank you. Leigh Carlson. Isn't that amazing? Collingwood Round 9, Fitzroy Round 10 and played well in both games. Got Brownlow votes for both clubs in the one season.

MARTY McMILLAN

It was big footy news midway through the 1974 season when Footscray captain David Thorpe walked out of the club demanding a trade to Richmond. The other side of the deal was 22-year-old Marty McMillan, who, just 18 months earlier, had played in a Grand Final. Marty had already played three games in the ones for the Tigers that season but was finding it hard to break into the side on a regular basis. It was certainly a strange time in footy when players could swap clubs midseason.

Richo: Marty, welcome to the Coodabeens.

Marty McMillan: Good to be here.

Richo: It's 1974, Richmond had a very powerful side but after seven or eight rounds you'd already played three senior games.

Marty McMillan: I thought I'd played a couple more actually but three sounds about right. I was playing pretty well but I just couldn't get a game because the side was so strong. At that stage, my old man knew a bloke at Hawthorn so I gave him a ring. And he said they were interested, but then Footscray rang up and the $15,000 started getting mentioned. And then all of a sudden I'm at Footscray.

Covey: Was the $15,000 for you or for the club?

Marty McMillan: The money was for Footscray and then I got a little bit of that to play.

Torch: You would have had to get petrol money, it's a long way from Mount Waverley to the Western Oval.

Marty McMillan: I worked in Camberwell and by the time I got there and got back home it was certainly a long way. That was why it never really worked—too much driving.

Covey: And just how much of a challenge was it to turn up midweek to a training session with these blokes you'd never met?

Marty McMillan: Well, I didn't even train. They told me to train at Richmond and come over to Footscray after training. So the first thing I saw was Kelvin Templeton walking out of the ground after training in his first year, and then I met a couple of Footscray blokes. Dick Collinson the president and Bob Rose were there and they said if you sign up now, we'll put you on a wing. I wasn't comfortable with that, I didn't want to put some other poor bloke out because that had happened to me. So I said, no, I'll just play in the seconds and then called Alan Schwab back at Richmond and he told me they couldn't do any better money wise so I should sign the deal.

Richo: And away you go. At this stage, you're 22 years of age, you've played in a Grand Final, so you must have thought, where is this going to go now having played in a Grand Final, the flag's so close?

Marty McMillan: Well, I didn't get a game in the '73 Grand Final. But I started off in the side in '74 so I thought I was a real chance to get going. And the next year at Footscray, I got a couple of Brownlow votes, so I was holding my own but I got a couple of injuries and ended up in the VFA playing for Geelong West because Billy Goggin took over as coach at the end of that year. So I ended up at Geelong West which is even further away!

Billy: That was a fairly strong team at Geelong West though Marty.

Marty McMillan: That year they lost six players out of the Premiership side and they got me. I wasn't going to make up for six of them because they were a pretty strong side. And it was enjoyable to play there as well.

Covey: And even if your time at Footscray was short-lived with only seven games, did you enjoy going out there?

Marty McMillan: I had a ball mate, they were a great bunch of blokes. The first week I was there, I played in the reserves, had a few beers after the game and I think I got home at 12.30.

Champs: And today Marty, are you a Tigers man or a Bulldogs man?

Marty McMillan: I still barrack for the Tiges because I started there in the Under 19s in 1970 and most blokes go back to the club they started at.

Covey: Did you ever get together with David Thorpe to discuss your role in footy history?

Marty McMillan: No, I ran into him playing in the reserves the next year and he said, 'We've come a long way Marty, haven't we?'

Richo: Thanks very much for joining us Marty.

Marty McMillan: Good on you boys.

Richo: Marty McMillan there, and how's that, he and David Thorpe running into each other in the reserves game the next year.

Covey: And we were using a as a primary reference source here an article from *The Age* of Friday, May 31, 1974, written by Ron Carter. He's written how the final clearance details were settled in a two-hour meeting between Richmond president Ian Wilson and Footscray president Dick Collinson.

Next par, Mr. Wilson returned from overseas only a few hours earlier—Octa's flown back to do the Marty McMillan, David Thorpe deal!

Torch: And talk about understatement, Thorpe wanted to go to Richmond and we fulfilled his request.

Covey: It does say that Footscray and Thorpe decided to part recently after Thorpe strongly criticised Bob Rose's coaching methods and said he wanted to be the Bulldogs coach. That's a fair claim!

GARY COWTON

When North Melbourne wanted a player in the late '70s, they more often than not got their man, no matter the cost. So, when Ron Barassi was set on bringing Footscray Brownlow Medallist Gary Dempsey across to Arden St, the cost was dual Premiership player, Gary Cowton. Crazy Horse reluctantly went to Footscray and then on to South Melbourne before landing back at North where he found himself playing with his replacement, Gary Dempsey.

Richo: Gary, welcome to the Coodabeens.

Gary Cowton: Thanks fellas, great to be with you.

Richo: Gary, it is an extraordinary career you had and players looking back on it now would pinch themselves to think that you could play in five Grand Finals in a row.

Gary Cowton: Well, I'll give you a little correction, it was six. Five years in a row and because of the drawn Grand Final, that makes it six.

Richo: It is quite amazing. But of course, all anyone is ever going to ask you about, and we're going to ask you now, is the sprays that you got from Barass.

Gary Cowton: I never got sprayed, I was just a cute country boy who did what he was told. No I had a couple of clashes with Barass, it was his way or no way as pretty much everybody knows, and the man got results. You had to listen and had to conform, otherwise you spent a couple of weeks out as I did a couple of times with not doing what he was asking properly.

Covey: Now, I have in front of me a copy of *The Age* newspaper from 23 February 1979 and it says 'Dempsey Swap Three For One'. It's written by Mike Sheahan and he's reported that you're one of the three players offered to Footscray in exchange for Gary Dempsey. Towards the finish, Ron Joseph is quoted as saying he knew nothing of the proposed swap, 'It's news to me,' he said. When did it become news to you?

Gary Cowton: I'm not sure of Ron's involvement in that one, but I'll just go back a little bit because I was a country kid from Benalla and just an innocent boy coming down to the big city to play with North Melbourne. My football grew with North Melbourne and as a loyal kid, it was in '77 was when I was first counted in swaps, this was before the Gary Dempsey trade and when I first heard it over the news or in the paper, I was absolutely gutted. Here I am, North Melbourne, North Melbourne, North Melbourne and next thing, they want to throw me to some other club. But I suppose it's a semi-backhanded compliment, if you're good enough within your own team or if you're good enough for another team that might want to use you or have a look at you. But I was just totally gutted.

Richo: It has to change your view of footy because you've come down to North Melbourne and they were the bridesmaids of the league and then you'd live through that incredibly exciting period where they turned all that around.

Gary Cowton: Incredibly exciting is totally correct, to go from the Shinboners, down for those couple of years where we won two games in my first year, one game in my second year, and then Barass came and turned everything around. It was definitely an exciting period for us as the players who stayed there, the ones Barass wanted to form into the Premiership teams. And obviously for our supporters it was an incredible time.

Covey: When you said you were incredibly gutted by that first mention of being a swap possibility in 1977. Did you convey that feeling to the club?

Gary Cowton: Yes, I did, but I quickly received a phone call from them saying don't worry about it, it's all just football stuff, you're secure and away you go, and that happened for two years in a row. Coming back to the newspaper article with *The Age* and Mike Sheahan, I didn't receive a phone call from North Melbourne saying don't worry about it, so I think the writing was on the wall wasn't it?

Richo: You were involved in the Gary Dempsey swap to Footscray and then you play the season at South is that right?

Gary Cowton: Not a full season. After having a couple of seasons at the Bulldogs with another fantastic coach, sorry, very much tongue in cheek, a guy from Richmond who could play a reasonable game or two but when he came across to the Bulldogs to coach we didn't see eye to eye, RH [Royce Hart] were his initials. So at that stage it was time to move.

Covey: You managed to play 40 games across the two years.

Gary Cowton: Yes, I played a full season, so I played the full 22 and then just a small injury the next year.

Richo: Then off to South and then the full circle, it must have been very satisfying to be able to finish your career back at North.

Gary Cowton: You're totally correct, it was in my blood growing up there. As I mentioned earlier, my football was growing up at North and I loved the players and the club and everything.

Billy: Were there many of the players still on the list who were there when you left, Gary?

Gary Cowton: Yes, there were still quite a few, it was nearly like a homecoming, which was good and even Demps was there so we swapped and then we ended up playing together.

Covey: And had you talked to him at all about the swap prior to then playing with him?

Gary Cowton: With Dempsey? No, not at all. Even in '83 when I was back there we didn't chat about it.

Covey: He could have bought you a beer.

Gary Cowton: Well, he probably could have afforded a beer whereas I couldn't. When he went to North I'm sure he ended up with much more than I did going to the Bulldogs.

Billy: Well, there were a few there on a decent whack over your time.

Gary Cowton: At North? Most definitely.

Billy: Who was the best of those players who came into the North side to get you into those finals? Who was the most inspirational?

Gary Cowton: We had a dual Brownlow Medallist who was already there. Blighty was one of the best and I think probably under mentioned a bit is Barry Davis. We got the three in the 10-year trade but Barry Davis was that unassuming character that was in everything and did everything. Then Barry Cable came back so we really recruited very excellently for the club, but they talk about Barass buying the Premiership but apart from the three 10-year players, which North was on top of and got in first and bought the right sort of players, a solid backman [John Rantall], a solid all-rounder in Barry Davis and our full forward Doug Wade, everybody else had the same opportunity. So in my mind there were three and then obviously after that Blighty came and other top players but they were all available to everybody else, weren't they?

Covey: Did you get paired up with Blighty in training drills?

Gary Cowton: No my pairing up was with the wonderful man who was hot and cold and could win games in his own hand. And that's Sam Kekovich. We were always manned up and he toughened me up pretty quickly and then I eventually got a few back on him.

Covey: And did he used to rave on like he does today?

Gary Cowton: In his own private corner he used to but no one would really listen to him! But I suppose with a TV camera, we've got to put up with him or we change channels.

Torch: And he was another country boy, but he wasn't obviously a quiet country boy.

Gary Cowton: Some people have a little bit of a different opinion about themselves but you've got to have characters in this world.

Covey: Exactly, well you are character yourself carrying the Crazy Horse mantle and dashing through the backline and bouncing the ball, we used to love you on the break. In that last year you played just the one game which left you with a career title of 199. Did you do enough to qualify for the 200 Club?

Gary Cowton: We were involved in those first night finals, so we were involved in many other games in the VFL and I did get my 200 Club membership.

Richo: Gary it has been wonderful talking to you this morning. Thank you so much.

Gary Cowton: Great to speak to you guys, I've been listening to you for years. Thanks.

Cult Figures

DANNIE SEOW

Dannie Seow was a Montmorency boy who graduated from the junior ranks to play league football for Collingwood. After just a couple of years and some serious concussion issues, he quit footy to attend high school and college in the USA. And then he returned to Melbourne for two more VFL seasons with the Demons to cap off an eventful 25-game senior career.

Richo: Our next guest was one of the first Asian Australians to play footy at the very highest level in Australian football. Joining us on line now from his home in Washington, DC, Dannie Seow.

Dannie Seow: Oh, thanks for the invitation guys.

Richo: Look, are you aware now at all this distance where you live in another country, what a cult player you were with young Collingwood supporters back in the day?

Dannie Seow: Not really. Maybe when I went to teach the kids at the primary school, the Asians would listen to me.

Richo: And tell us a bit about that, people were aware at the time that you were an Asian Australian. Tell us about your family background, Dannie.

Dannie Seow: Well, my father was Chinese. He was born in

Singapore. I'm a bit of a mutt, I would say on the Chinese side, too, because my grandmother was from Beijing and my grandfather from Xiamen, which is in the southeast corner of China, the closest point to Taiwan. And my mother is Spanish/Scottish/Irish with my grandmother being from Glasgow.

Billy: But Collingwood picked you up from Montmorency.

Dannie Seow: Yes, Under 14s. They stole me.

Billy: So, did you come up through the Under 19s?

Dannie Seow: Yes, Keith Burns was the coach then.

Richo: Did Keith spot you playing for Monty?

Dannie Seow: There was a guy named Dennis Le Gassick actually and he and Keith approached me at a local game and said, Oh, you're coming and training with us for pre-season now. And I was 14 at the time. And I didn't believe them.

Torch: And what did you parents say?

Dannie Seow: It was my mother and I just told her I'm doing it and she said great. And my grandmother was over the moon because she was crazy Collingwood.

Covey: At 14 years of age did you catch the train from Montmorency to training?

Dannie Seow: Yeah, every time. Forty-five minutes to training. And there were times you actually wouldn't pay at the station. We'd jump the train because we didn't have any money.

Champs: Well, Dannie, we find that entertaining because the train to Monty still carries feral Pies fans every Friday night to games at the 'G on the Hurstbridge line.

Dannie Seow: Oh, that's nice to know but it's not the red rattler anymore though, is it?

Richo: It's not red. It's mostly sort of silver with a little blue and red down the side. Tell us who some of your teammates were in the Under 19s back then at Collingwood.

Dannie Seow: Oh, Neville Shaw, Fatui Ataata, a couple of guys I used to actually play with at Montmorency High School, we had a few guys at Collingwood at the time such as Owen Davies. There were a few other guys like Gavin Crosisca just coming in when I left, I think I was already in the ones then when Gav came in, and also Gavin Brown.

Billy: What do you recall of your first game, Dannie?

Dannie Seow: My first senior game was against Carlton and I came off the bench, I played on Peter Dean and I immediately discovered how much quicker it was. I just thought this will be fine, I'll be fine.

Richo: And who was coaching the Pies that day?

Dannie Seow: It was Leigh Matthews. Leigh had just come in. Bobby Rose was the coach at the time, and then they replaced him with Leigh Matthews who changed everything for the club.

Covey: We just talked about how Collingwood invited you down when you were 14, but you are gone after just two seasons of senior footy. What happened?

Dannie Seow: I retired. No, what happened was I ended up having severe concussion. It was in a practice game and I hit heads with another guy. I was actually told that I was okay to keep playing so I kept playing over the weeks and what happened was I ended up just really flat, but I thought I was only sick, just got a flu or something. And then we played a practice match two weeks later against Fitzroy and suddenly, I was fine. I was playing fine and then we went into the season. And we play against Hawthorn again, I think it was, and that was fine up until maybe 15 or 20 minutes into the first quarter. And then, suddenly, I just had pressure on my brain,

I couldn't breathe, I was short of breath, I had nausea, blurred vision and I asked Leigh to take me off. But then I looked over and we already had two guys on the bench who couldn't come on for the rest of the game so I had to stay on and hold on to Russell Morris' jumper.

Richo: And that was your last game for Collingwood?

Dannie Seow: No, I didn't play a good game and I got dropped but then I was more determined to come back and I kept playing which I probably shouldn't have. And I ended up getting scans on my own or getting an ECG done and things like that. And the MRI CAT scan didn't show anything. The ECG actually showed that I had abnormal electrolysis in the brain and that really caused me to stop playing. And then I thought, well, I hadn't finished my high school yet because I actually left school at 15 for football, so I went back. And that's how I ended up in America. I wanted to go and finish high school in America.

Covey: And then in '88 you came back and played for two seasons at Melbourne?

Dannie Seow: I actually got accepted at a few colleges and went and played American football at North Carolina, and played receiver and strong safety, that was a lot of fun.

Richo: Dannie that's extraordinary with your story of your concussion as a teenager 30 years ago. And now what's coming out in American football which you also played.

Dannie Seow: Yes, people look at me strangely when I say after concussion I played American football. They said what were you doing and I said I don't know, I was reckless.

Richo: You were a cult figure in the VFL, Pies supporters loved you, Dannie.

Dannie Seow: I must say that the Collingwood supporters were really great. Melbourne supporters were good as well but the

Collingwood supporters especially because I grew up there, they were fantastic. Even from when I was a young age to getting to a little older, they were always great. After training you'd be coming out of the rooms and they're still there just waiting for you. I'd always be the last one to leave and they'd be always there waiting for you to sign something and tell you something and they're really quite amazing, the Collingwood supporters. I think they helped the team especially when I was playing, to get through games to win, particularly some finals games. We'd kick a goal and everyone would cheer but it wouldn't stop, the spectators would just keep roaring and there was just like this constant wave of emotion and sound coming from the Collingwood supporters. Whether they were chanting 'Collingwood' or whatever they're doing, more than any other team, Collingwood supporters at the time were just amazing.

Billy: And do you still follow the Pies from afar Dannie?

Dannie Seow: Oh, yes, always. I've been Collingwood since I was five, so I can't get rid of that.

Richo: Well, Dannie, it has been wonderful talking to you. I shudder to think what time of night it is there in Washington, DC so we'll let you get back to sleep. Thanks for your time.

Dannie Seow: Great to speak to you guys and thank you for having me.

Richo: Dannie Seow. Plucked out of Montmorency High to play for Collingwood and now running his own company in Washington DC.

Covey: And all those fans waiting outside the rooms for Dannie didn't need to wait. They could talk to him on the train on the way home!

AUSTIN McCRABB

Austin McCrabb is one of the AFL/VFL all-time great cult figures. We spoke to him as a player with a foot in both camps.

Richo: G'day Austin, where do we find you this morning?

Austin McCrabb: I'm actually in Clifton Hill at the moment. It was a bit like that song Champs sings [Train to Montmorency] because I came in on that train this morning to pick up my car. I live out Eltham way but there were no Collingwood supporters on the train this morning, I think they're all asleep.

Covey: So why didn't you ride your bike in to get the car?

Austin McCrabb: I've got a perfectly good bike at home, but I don't tend to ride it that much anymore on the road. I do other things to keep fit these days.

Covey: Austin, you're famous for one particular bike ride you took during your playing days?

Austin McCrabb: Yeah, that's right when I was about 20 I rode my bike across to Perth. I suppose that's the one you're talking about Coves?

Covey: Didn't you go to Perth and then on up to Darwin?

Austin McCrabb: That's right. Yeah.

Richo: People who do long rides now have lots of equipment and support crew and the like, but what did you take with you on your bike ride?

Austin McCrabb: Not a great deal. And I sort of believe in traveling fairly light, really. So just a very small little sleeping bag and a ground sheet and that's about it. I wasn't all loaded up like you see a lot of the touring cyclists these days. I believe in trying to go as far as possible each day which meant I had to be as light as I could.

Billy: And no lycra I'm guessing?

Austin McCrabb: No, just footy shorts!

Covey: What about on the personal hygiene side of things? You took a couple of items didn't you?

Austin McCrabb: Only a couple of pairs of jocks. And, look, there wasn't really a great need for personal hygiene because I was out there all by myself.

Billy: Your mother said you took a toothbrush and deodorant.

Austin McCrabb: Did she really? Well mum would know, wouldn't she? I must have but I didn't really have a big requirement for the personal hygiene part of it.

Covey: Were you playing at Geelong at the time or was that before you played at the Cats?

Austin McCrabb: No, yeah, it was before I played at Geelong, I was playing back at Colac-Coragulac and I'd missed the year with a broken arm. So I thought I'll go for a bit of a ride in about October.

Champs: And the machine you chose for your trip was it an up-to-date, latest model.

Austin McCrabb: It was a Cecil Walker model from a shop in Elizabeth Street and I bought my bike there. It was just a racing bike, a normal 10-speed.

Billy: So how did you end up down at the Cats a couple of years later, Austin?

Austin McCrabb: Bill McMaster asked me down, he was the recruiting manager. There was no draft or anything like that back then. But Colac was zoned to Fitzroy actually, but I went to Fitzroy for the Under 19s for a bit before that and played a year there. Then I went back to Colac. And then a lot of local Western District guys used to get asked down to Geelong and went down to try it out. I was lucky enough to get a few games.

Billy: And John Devine would have picked you for your very first game.

Austin McCrabb: That's right, John was the coach there for two years before Malcolm [Blight] came along.

Covey: Did he have a soft spot for you? Because he came from Colac?

Austin McCrabb: Maybe he did! Yes. I'm very grateful to John for giving me a go. That's for sure.

Champs: And you also played under Malcolm?

Austin McCrabb: That's right. Malcolm came down and I was there for three years under Malcolm.

Champs: And how was that experience?

Austin McCrabb: It was pretty good. Malcolm was a good coach but we all sort of know about Malcolm and the way he is. He got a lot out of the players there and was reasonably successful without winning the ultimate prize.

Covey: And, of course, just like the bike ride gets brought

WELL I TOLD AUSTIN TO USE A DEODORANT!
3
9

up all the time with you, so does the day at Waverley against Hawthorn.

Austin McCrabb: Yes, well, I suppose I should thank Malcolm for doing that to me, shouldn't I, because it's the sort of the thing that people want to ask me about.

Covey: So what happened?

Austin McCrabb: I just think he wasn't happy with me to put it mildly. And when he came out at quarter-time he decided that I didn't deserve to be in the huddle. So, he made me stand outside the huddle. Which sounds really ridiculous, but that's what happened.

Champs: How did that feel at the time?

Austin McCrabb: I'd been playing quite well so it didn't really worry me too much. Actually, the people in the crowd thought that the reason I was standing out of the huddle was because I'd been playing so well. They thought I was the only one that deserved to be in a huddle by myself and the others had to go over with him.

Covey: It was like Malcolm was saying 'Look at McCrabb over here, he's done everything, right!'

Austin McCrabb: That's exactly right. And he didn't drag me. So that was a good thing but, look, he had his funny little ways. He liked to do things this way and he didn't want to get bogged down in boredom, Malcolm. He liked sort of changing things up a bit. That's fair enough.

Billy: How did you finish your days at Geelong and get to Hawthorn?

Austin McCrabb: Well, they sacked me basically! And I was lucky enough to get picked up by Hawthorn. So I went in the draft, the draft was around then. I remember I was watching the cricket at the MCG when the World Cup was on and I think my mum might've rung me and said, 'You've been drafted by Hawthorn,' so I thought I'd better go to training then. So I went up there and that was good, they were a great club, Hawthorn, I really enjoyed being there for a couple of years.

Covey: Did your mum ring up and say: 'You've been drafted by Hawthorn Have you got your toothbrush and your deodorant stick, dear?'

Austin McCrabb: Yeah, jump on your bike and get up to Glenferrie.

Billy: Did they draft you because they had a specific role for you?

Austin McCrabb: I don't know. I think most people would probably ask that question as well, why they would have drafted me but they did pick me up. They picked up Ricky Nixon as well at the same time and he and I were the big recruits for that year.

Covey: And, of course, they were a Premiership side, you went to a side that had just won the flag.

Austin McCrabb: That's right, yeah. I came from a fairly good side in Geelong and went to a really good side at Hawthorn. And all the good players were still there. So it was a good club to go to.

Covey: Do you still go down and watch the Cats, Austin?

Austin McCrabb: Look, I'm going tonight and I sometimes get into the MCG to see them when they come to Melbourne. I love watching them, they're great. I'm definitely still a Cats man.

Richo: Fantastic. Great to have you on the Coodabeens this morning, Austin.

Austin McCrabb: Thanks, guys.

Champs: And stay away from that Monty train!

KATRINA MORRIS

For over 100 years, every official to grace a VFL/AFL ground was male. That all changed in 1998 when Katrina Presley blazed a trail as the first female goal umpire in the big leagues. It took some effort to get there, but Katrina became a fixture at Gabba matches in Brisbane for four years. The former umpire, now Katrina Morris, joined us in 2016 to reminisce.

Richo: Katrina Presley, now Katrina Morris, joins us.

Katrina Morris: Good morning.

Richo: Tell us what you're doing now with your life and with sport and footy.

Katrina Morris: Okay, well, actually, I've walked away from football. I'm a mum of three children. My eldest turns 11 this year and I've got two daughters and a son. And my six-year-old son has just signed up to play Auskick.

Billy: Wonderful, which Auskick?

Katrina Morris: Auskick at Jimboomba. With the Redbacks.

Covey: So you've hung up the flags?

Katrina Morris: Yes, I have. I figured when I fell pregnant with Charlotte, that it probably wasn't a good idea to be standing in the goals and having someone the size of Tony Lockett running through me.

Billy: Did you get collected at any stage in your four years behind the white line Katrina?

Katrina Morris: I got collected a couple of times in the local leagues. In the AFL, I got collected by a boundary umpire of all things!

Billy: Friendly fire.

Katrina Morris: He wasn't watching where he was going. And he ran straight through me. I ended up on the ground and he got cut. So it worked out well!

Richo: Katrina, your debut as a goal umpire at the highest level of the AFL didn't just throw into focus the participation of women at the highest level, but also on the very peculiar art that is the goal umpire. Most people don't give it much mind and when they do, they think, 'Oh, that couldn't be that hard. I could do that.' But it's only when you actually do it, you realise how hard it is.

Katrina Morris: You've got to try and remain focused the whole time, your concentration levels have to be high, you can't take your eye off the football because you just don't know what's going to happen.

Richo: And it happens so quickly.

Katrina Morris: It does happen very quickly. In my first game, within the first 10 seconds the ball was down my end. And I was like, 'Holy snap and duck poo, okay?' It moves a bit quicker up at this level than it does at the lower level. But you have all the training and you're prepared for it but you've got to be fast. So you've got to train and do a lot of exercises to be speedy. It is a lot more than just standing in the goals and going 'Oh, yeah'.

Covey: How long was it between when you first waved the flags at a local level, and doing your first AFL game?

Katrina Morris: Ten years.

Covey: That's a lot of flag waving.

Katrina Morris: That is a lot of flag waving. I'd done a senior Grand Final up here in Queensland before that. There were a number of guys who had come on to the goal umpires list in Queensland and then all of a sudden, they were up there on the AFL list within two years. So it took me 10 years to get there.

Billy: I was just wondering, did you have your own flags that you took to and from the ground or did each ground have flags for you?

Katrina Morris: We had our own. We were all very professional and had our own kit. There were times that we forgot to bring them with us because we were having a stupid day and we'd have a set somewhere but it was all part of our own kit. We had our own footy boots and our own uniforms, nothing was provided to us, we had to get it ourselves.

Champs: You'd have to make your own flags did you out of an old broom stick and some calico?

Katrina Morris: Yes we did! But we didn't use broomsticks though some of us used dowel to start off with. But later on, it came down that they were able to get some PVC piping ones made up for us professionally. And they were just two pieces that were slotted together, you had your flags, and you had shoelaces attached to the bottom of them and you just tied them on and then got there with your electrical tape.

Torch: Katrina these days there's talk about umpires being fully professional. How did you manage working and trying to be a senior goal umpire at the same time?

Katrina Morris: I was working a full-time job with the Commonwealth Bank at the time as a conveyancing officer. We only had official training as a group twice a week. But then we were expected to do our own training on top of that, so I was training four hours a day. And that was just me because that's what I wanted to do. Four hours a day as well as doing my full-time job and then football on weekends.

Richo: In the time since you broke through to the senior level the goals and goal umpiring had changed in all sorts of subtle ways with more padding on the posts, the point posts are as high as the goal posts used to be maybe 25 years ago, the goal umpires' uniforms have become much more athletic, no more standing there wearing the grocer's dust coat. From your point of view, what changes are the most important, and can you see room for any more changes?

Katrina Morris: When I was leaving football, the coats were gone. But look, the posts being a bit higher made the goal umpire's job easier to be quite honest. Because not that we were guessing and we'd be in the right position to be under the flight, but it takes away that scepticism from commentators and spectators around whether the ball would have hit the post.

Richo: Yes, I can tell from up here. I know better than the umpire.

Katrina Morris: Of course, everybody does! The uniforms make things that little bit easier for you to get around in. They're not so good when it's wet, rainy and cold. But the basics of it all hasn't really changed that much. You've still got to be in the right spot. You've got to know football.

Billy: But there is talk of maybe introducing a second goal umpire. Have you got a view on that?

Katrina Morris: Oh, that's stupid. Sorry. We tried that in trial games in the pre-season cup many years ago up in Cairns where we did trial the two-goal umpire system. And if you don't have a really good working relationship with that other goal umpire, you can get in all sorts of trouble. There was four of us on the list at the time so we already knew which pair would be at each end so we'd work out okay, one doing the goal for this one the other doing the behind. But they'd want to do a hell of a lot of research into it and they'd want to get in there and have a real good go at it and say, these are the guidelines, this is what you should do. Otherwise, there's going to be all sorts of trouble.

Covey: You blazed the trail that has been followed by Chelsea Roffey, who's behind the goals now and has done a Grand Final. When Chelsea graduated to the AFL ranks, did she give you a call for some advice?

Katrina Morris: Well I went out and saw Chelsea when she was a school umpire in school footy. My first year I had to go out and watch her and give her some pointers. And then she came and joined us the year after. So I've known Chelsea for quite a few years. And we all had our own mentors at that stage and she had Glen Drieberg as a mentor when she first went on. Glen was the man on the spot for Chels. And it would have been better for her to have him than it would have been for me because her experience was completely different to mine.

Covey: Because you started in 1998 as did goal umpire David Dixon. And he breaks the all-time AFL games record today in the match between Collingwood and St Kilda.

Katrina Morris: Isn't that the most awesome thing? He's a really nice bloke too.

Torch: What were some of the highlights you goal umpired Katrina?

Katrina Morris: I was behind the goals for a lot of things. I was under the goals when Michael Voss launched a 70-metre kick for goal. There's been lots of things that have been lots of fun, really good memories. And some fabulous things that you see as a goal umpire because, hey, you can't get a better seat in the house.

Covey: When you were goal umpiring and someone did unload a 70-metre bomb like Vossy and you know the cameras are on you and the crowds are looking at you, did you sometimes just delay your signal to really build the tension and the excitement?

Katrina Morris: No. There's no need for that everybody knew who I was by that stage, I was the one wanting to go and hide somewhere. Anytime they mentioned my name, I knew I was going to get into trouble somewhere.

Billy: And did you ever report anyone Katrina?

Katrina Morris: Not in the AFL but in lower leagues, of course. There's lots of things that need to be done back in the lower level. But no, in the AFL I didn't get to do that because there was nothing really going on.

Richo: Katrina it's been tremendous talking with you this morning. Thank you very much.

Katrina Morris: You're welcome. Thank you for calling.

Richo: A true trailblazer there Katrina Morris better known to people as Katrina Presley when she burst onto the scene as the first woman umpire at the very highest level in the AFL.

ROCHFORD DEVENISH-MEARES

One of the most popular requests from listeners over the years has been to track down the man with the best name the game has ever heard: Rochford Devenish-Meares. Well, they asked and we got him in 2013! Rochford played eight games for Hawthorn in 1968 and later crossed to Geelong where he failed to make a senior appearance.

Covey: Great to have you on the show because Billy and I are big Geelong fans and we remember you being down there and we often refer to you as one of the great hyphenated names in football, Rochford.

Rochford Devenish-Meares: Well, that's my only claim to fame Basically, I played a few games but, because of my name, I was remembered by everyone.

Richo: So, tell us about your footy career and how you got to Hawthorn?

Rochford Devenish-Meares: I was a kid at Launceston Grammar School and I got approached by a couple of sides,

Melbourne, I think, St Kilda looked at me and Hawthorn and we decided to go with Hawthorn, and I came across and went to Trinity Grammar for a year and they wouldn't let me play League football. I was almost kicked out of school for playing one game in the reserves against St Kilda.

Richo: How did you talk your way out of that?

Rochford Devenish-Meares: I don't know how I did it, it, I used a fair bit of BS, I suppose.

Billy: Who was coaching the Hawks at that time, Rochford?

Rochford Devenish-Meares: Peter O'Donohue was coaching the first year I went across. And then, of course, Kanga [John Kennedy] came on board in '68 and made the difference for Hawthorn and it went on from there.

Covey: And you played eight games in that year. Did you play around the middle of the ground?

Rochford Devenish-Meares: I came across as a forward from Tasmania and I came across in the same year as Huddo [Peter Hudson]. And Kanga said to me, the best way to make you a good forward is to become a good backman first. The first game I was playing against South Melbourne. I played on Paul Harrison who I wasn't aware was a bit of a tough nut and I was dropped into the full back position five minutes before the game because Ian Bremner was injured. And Kanga came to me and said, you're playing full back and I just about wet myself.

Torch: Was that the drawn game, that game at Glenferrie? I remember that game because Bobby Skilton got cleaned up and they've gone to take him off on a stretcher and he got up again and kicked five goals.

Rochford Devenish-Meares: Graeme John had taken a mark and I ran out and he just stopped and I just ran into him about 20 metres out from the goals. And I just ran through him, unintentionally, I just kept going I wasn't intending to hit him. Anyway, a big blue started, I think Graeme John got knocked out. And then all of a sudden, Skilton, who as you said had been knocked out just a little while before, I've got his arm around my neck and he's putting me in a choker hold.

Covey: Bobby Skilton! He won the Brownlow in '68, you could've cost him the medal!

Richo: Rochford, you mentioned that your first year was also the first year that the great Peter Hudson also came across from Tassie. You were from the north, he was from the south, were you aware of his abilities before you came across?

Rochford Devenish-Meares: Absolutely, he was a champion. I was very aware and, of course, it was very exciting to get Peter Hudson in there because he was such an incredible footballer. You just had to pump the ball anywhere within about 50 metres of him and he would get it.

Richo: It was almost miraculous watching him, wasn't it?

Rochford Devenish-Meares: It was, yeah. Coming off the half-back flank, you could just bang it down there and Huddo one out would get the ball 75-80% of the time.

Covey: Did he do much a training?

Rochford Devenish-Meares: He wasn't a great trainer. He was one of those guys, he was a big guy and had a big backside. And he had incredible speed over the first couple of metres. He was so quick for a big bloke.

Covey: So, Rochford, how did you find your way to Geelong?

Rochford Devenish-Meares: Well, long story, I finished up that '68 season with an injury and I didn't play the last few games. Anyway, being a young bloke, I was 19 at the time, I met a girl from Geelong and I finished up being sidetracked a little bit. I played a couple of practice games in '69 with Hawthorn. And then I started to miss a few training sessions. I was staying in Moorabbin and David Parkin used to drive across and pick me up for pre-season in the morning. I didn't have a car at the time. And he would pick me up and drive me back to Marcellin College and we used to do commando cross-training down on the river.

Billy: And why the Cats, Rochford?

Rochford Devenish-Meares: Well, the secretary at the time heard I was living in Geelong and the girl I was going out with, her father was a policeman. And he said the club had got in touch with him inviting me to come on down and have a run. And they were my favourite side as a kid.

Covey: And they gave you Denis Marshall's No. 2 after he had left.

Rochford Devenish-Meares: I was that chuffed to be given the No. 2. I played a couple of reserves games in '69 and I figured in 1970 in the pre-season, I did pretty well on in the pre-season training and practice games. And Peter Pianto told me at three-quarter time in the last practice game, he said you're in the side against Hawthorn next week on a half-back flank. But I got a bit enthusiastic and ran into a pack and broke my arm in a couple of places.

Billy: Obviously it took a while to come back from that broken arm and things weren't quite the same for your career thereafter.

Rochford Devenish-Meares: I was working up in Melbourne and the secretary Terry Hogan said they'd got a clearance from Hawthorn that cost them a couple of thousand dollars or something, and so Geelong wouldn't release me. I knew Shane Molloy who played for Fitzroy, he used to work at the same company I worked for, and he said come down and have a run. So, I went down to Fitzroy and had a couple of practice sessions and I just wasn't very interested. And my family had moved across to Western Australia and Dad said come across and work in the west, it's the land of adventure and freedom and blond-haired men and fine-looking women. So, I left Melbourne and went across to Western Australia and Subiaco got a clearance for me. And I played with Subi for the next eight or nine years.

Covey: And who do you barrack for these days Rochford, Geelong?

Rochford Devenish-Meares: My preference is Hawthorn, obviously, I'm a business man here in Perth and I'm almost retired now. And I've got a soft spot for the Dockers, I'd love to see the Dockers get up and win a flag.

Richo: You've got plenty of interest in this year's final series.

Covey: Do you still see Denis Marshall around Perth at all?

Rochford Devenish-Meares: He goes down to the Mosman Park Bowling Club quite a lot and I've been meaning to go in and catch up with him.

Covey: You could start with 'I took over your jumper, Denis!'

Rochford Devenish-Meares: Funnily enough, I was over in Melbourne a few weeks ago and and I rang up the Hawthorn footy club to get a couple of tickets to the past players and Peter Knights rang me back and said, 'Did you know I took your number when you left? You had No. 24 before I took it'.

Torch: We mentioned Huddo but the other full forward you would have ended up with at Subi was Austin Robertson Jr. who kicked more goals in his first season than Huddo did in his first season.

Rochford Devenish-Meares: He was tremendous. I played in the '73 Grand Final side with Austin at Subi and we just recently had our 40-year reunion. Mike Fitzpatrick and Brian Sierakowski and Dennis Blair and all the boys were there and it was tremendous.

Covey: It's great to be acquainted with you for the first time. Thanks for joining us this morning.

Rochford Devenish-Meares: Lovely to talk to you.

Oh Brother, Oh Sister!

BELINDA BOWEY

Women's footy has leapt to prominence in recent seasons with the formation of AFLW but a trail was blazed many years earlier by the likes of Belinda Bowey in the VWFL. And what a trail it was! Belinda was a special guest on our radio show on the eve of her 350th game which was to be played at the St Kilda Sharks' famous home ground, the Peanut Farm.

Richo: Congratulations on 350 games, Belinda, it must seem almost unbelievable. Can you remember back to your first game?

Belinda Bowey: I can actually remember back to the phone call that I got asking to come down to play in a women's team.

Richo: Who rang you up?

Belinda Bowey: Charlie Hope, the junior coach who used to coach me when I was playing with the boys. And he rang me up and said, Oh, Belinda, we're starting a women's team and can you play. And I'm like, absolutely. I'd actually been called by another team a couple of weeks earlier and I said, look, I'm sorry, I'm in Year 12, it's a really busy year, blah, blah, blah, can't play. And then Charlie rings me up and says St Kilda is starting a team, can you play and I said, absolutely. And I was down there like a rocket.

Richo: Did you have a gap between playing mixed footy in boys' teams and you would have had a period when you weren't allowed to play at all?

Belinda Bowey: Well, it was Under 12s when I wasn't allowed to play anymore, the club just said 'Look, sorry, you're developing as a female you're not allowed to play footy anymore, you can't play with the boys'. So, that was pretty disappointing because those boys were my friends and it was great to play with them, I was playing with my twin brother. I just wasn't allowed to play footy anymore, that was it.

Billy: What was your original junior club?

Belinda Bowey: That was St Kilda City. So, I've been with St Kilda practically all my life other than just a couple of years with Keysborough. I played junior footy at St. Kilda and then women's footy at St Kilda, so the red, white and black have certainly been my colours of choice.

Covey: The 350 games Belinda, does that include the games at Keysborough?

Belinda Bowey: Yes, it does.

Covey: But it would be 300-plus at St Kilda, wouldn't it?

Belinda Bowey: I looked at it the other day and I played 45 for Keysborough in three years there so 305 if you want to say for St Kilda but that doesn't include junior matches, and I have no idea what junior matches take me to.

Billy: Your fitness must be pretty terrific, you mustn't have missed too many games, I wouldn't think in that space of time to rack up 350.

Belinda Bowey: Yeah, I've been really lucky in that I haven't had any major injuries. A lot of great players have, unfortunately, missed seasons, because they've done knees and, touch wood, hopefully I don't run out on Sunday and fall over and do my knee. But I've been really lucky and I haven't missed a season.

Champs: How much footy have you still got in you?

Belinda Bowey: Well, at the start of the year, I was like, OK, I'm going to play my 350 and then finish the season and I'll be done. But then I went back and played my first game this year and kind of went, Oh, I got a fair bit of the ball and I feel alright and I'm still getting a kick and so I think as long as I'm still making a difference to the team and can still help and not sit on the bench and just make up the numbers, I think I'll keep playing. I've got a couple of years left, the motivation to get to training when it's cold and wet and windy is a lot harder when you're older and you've got a lot of excuses, like business and staying where it's nice and warm. So, that's a little bit harder to get to training but on game day it's just amazing.

Billy: Irregardless (sic) of form, I suppose with that experience, your presence would be invaluable to the junior players in the team as a role model and a mentor.

Belinda Bowey: Yeah, absolutely. And just helping them with technique and being in the right position and knowing where the ball is going next, which is something you can't teach, you just know where the ball is gonna go even when you don't have position or your team doesn't have position. That's something that's really important out on the ground to help guide players into space and being that next option to get the ball.

Covey: Apart from that stuff you're doing at the Sharks, you also have an official capacity as an assistant coach at the Sandy Dragons.

Belinda Bowey: Yes, the TAC is a pathway for junior footballers to go into the VFLW and then into the AFLW. So, these girls are from 15 to 18, some are 19, playing football and the talent that is coming through is outstanding to watch. Women's football is just going to explode, it's really quite amazing some of the talent among these girls and they're a lot fitter and younger and faster so it's really exciting.

Covey: Do you think they're getting faster Belinda or perhaps…?

Belinda Bowey: Maybe I'm getting slower!

Covey: You said it, Belinda! And people wanting to know which one is Belinda, if they don't see you run through the banner, you're in the St Kilda jumper and what number are you wearing?

Belinda Bowey: I wear No. 18.

Covey: And who also wore 18 for St Kilda in the men's footy?

Belinda Bowey: That would be Brett Bowey, my brother.

Champs: Terrific!

Belinda Bowey: And I'm actually playing with my niece this weekend. It's a funny story she was born the Thursday after we won our first Grand Final so I've been playing footy in her whole life.

Covey: Belinda, you've been there for the whole journey for women's footy in what's been an historic time. You were playing when you had to stop playing when you were 12 and you've seen that change and now you've racked up 350 games. As you just said a few moments ago, women's footy is about to explode but that brings with it a whole lot of challenges. You're involved at the junior development area, if there's one thing the League could do that can just help this whole women's footy thing grow as it should, what would you get them to do?

Belinda Bowey: I guess ground availability and club rooms. A lot of times, even with the Sandy Dragons, one day we train here and then another day we train at another ground. There just doesn't seem to be enough grounds. But, in saying that as well, the league has been amazing, all the people behind the scenes, I can't play 350 games without all those people behind the scenes to make it happen. They've done all the hard work and I think what the league is doing is fantastic, women's football is amazing, more people know about it. Previously when I was playing and I'd say I play women's football, people would go, 'Really?' Now people go, 'Oh, do you know such and such' and they actually know women that are playing football now and follow it and see their progress and it's just fantastic. It's really amazing.

Richo: It's very exciting, Belinda. Congratulations again to you. And we know Gil [McLachlan] listens to the show, so more grounds and more clubrooms please, Gil. Have a tremendous day tomorrow. Enjoy the rest of the season.

Belinda Bowey: Thank you very much. Thanks, guys.

PETER RUSCUKLIC

Fitzroy fans were salivating at the prospect that their high-flying full forward, Alex Ruscuklic, had a brother who was seven years younger and was rumoured to be just as good. Peter Ruscuklic's VFL career didn't pan out the way he, and they, had hoped, but he became a goal-kicking phenomenon in the Sydney AFL, even breaking the mythical 200-goal-season mark in 1981.

Richo: Peter, welcome to the Coodabeens.

Peter Ruscuklic: Good morning.

Billy: Peter, you played for Fitzroy and Geelong, did you then head straight up to the Sydney Australian footy league?

Peter Ruscuklic: Not quite, I went from Fitzroy to Geelong and then got horse traded to South Australia for a year. I played with South Adelaide in 1977 under Haydn Bunton which was pretty good—I think I had started maturing by that stage.

Billy: So Geelong got rid of you too early.

Peter Ruscuklic: Probably a year or two too early.

Billy: Who was the coach then at the Geelong team, was it Olsson?

Peter Ruscuklic: That's right, Rod Olsson.

Billy: He couldn't find a spot for you regularly in the team?

Peter Ruscuklic: It might have been a combination of that and being a little bit immature.

Richo: Peter, tell us about your days as a junior coming up when Alex was a genuine star at the Lions and you're coming through behind him. What was that like?

Peter Ruscuklic: It was pretty daunting because the expectations were there. Everybody thought that the second brother would probably be better which was a bit of a challenge.

Covey: I remember people saying that Alex Ruscuklic has a brother who's twice as good.

Peter Ruscuklic: That sort of thing. It put unnecessary pressure on me but I realised that after I matured a little bit.

Richo: Tell us about your early days at Fitzroy. Did you come through the Under 19s?

Peter Ruscuklic: I did. I started off in the Under 19s, I came from the Diamond Valley from McLeod Rosanna over to the Fitzroy Under 19s and I played there a season, that was '73, when I was 18. And then I played most of the reserves season in '74 and '75 was the year that I played my first game with Fitzroy.

Covey: And did you like going for speccies just like Alex?

Peter Ruscuklic: No, I left that for him.

Richo: What was the scene like at Fitzroy in '75 Peter? Where was your home?

Peter Ruscuklic: The Junction Oval, a magnificent ground.

Richo: It's a long way from McLeod-Rosanna down to St Kilda though.

Peter Ruscuklic: It was hard to get the train down there as a kid.

Torch: And you had Kevin Rose as your coach at that time, how did you find Kevin, because he came from the enemy really as a Collingwood man.

Peter Ruscuklic: He was alright. Moving on from there, Hadyn Bunton was probably the person that started maturing me as a player.

Billy: Peter, in your first year down there at the at the Lions you picked up a Brownlow vote in one of your eight games. That was a feather in your cap and in your last year of VFL football the Cats even though they had to let you go, they thought so much of you that they held on to your number until Gary Ablett Jr. came along and they've given the Peter Ruscuklic 29 to him. That's a feather in your cap also!

Peter Ruscuklic: Oh good, well I see it that way too! I was No. 55 and then then got 29 on default. I think they lost the No. 55, so I wore 29.

Covey: We note those three seasons you had in Sydney, Peter, where you kicked 136 goals, 156 and then 213 in a season.

Peter Ruscuklic: That's right, I played at centre-half-forward for the first two seasons and the last season played at full forward. Remember, the grounds up there are quite compact. They're almost converted from a rugby league ground.

Covey: What was your biggest haul in one game in that 213 goal season?

Peter Ruscuklic: I had a three-week-spell of 24, 22 and 21.

Champs: Well, that would explain it.

Richo: Who were you playing for Peter?

Peter Ruscuklic: East Sydney. Alex was actually the coach in the first season.

Richo: Tell us about the Sydney league back then, this is going back quite a while. Who were the other players, both at East Sydney with you and any in the opposition teams? Where did they draw them from?

Peter Ruscuklic: Predominantly they were from Western Australia. A few locals but very few from South Australia and Victoria.

Richo: Peter, what's your involvement with footy nowadays?

Peter Ruscuklic: None, I just follow it and I just like to see a good game. I finished up coaching Myrtleford in '84 and '85 and the year before that I was assistant coach when Ablett was up there in '83. And I coached them in '84 and played about three seasons after that, and that was it. No more involvement.

Richo: And when you're watching the AFL as it is today, who do you barrack for Peter?

Peter Ruscuklic: Oh, whoever's on top. And that's Geelong at the moment obviously, Brisbane a few years ago, so I'm a turncoat.

Richo: So you haven't got that firm club allegiance any more?

Peter Ruscuklic: No. As I said, I do like a really good game.

Champs: Just back on Ablett at Myrtleford, how dominant was he in that comp?

Peter Ruscuklic: Well, needless to say, head and shoulders above everyone, I think he played something like eight games and in the Morris Medal, came fourth. He was just unbelievable.

Richo: Well, Peter, thanks so much. It's been terrific talking to you. And yes, you're one of those people who just enjoys a good game of football.

Peter Ruscuklic: That's it!

Covey: Well, you might be the first person we've talked to who's kick more than 200 goals in a season.

Richo: That those three weeks 22, 24 and 21.

Peter Ruscuklic: What I was really annoyed about though, with the 213, I missed five games.

Covey: You could've kicked 300!

Richo: Peter, thank you so much for joining us.

Peter Ruscuklic: Goodo, thank you, all the best.

Peter Ruscuklic sadly passed away suddenly in 2014 at the age of 58.

PAUL WYND

In the late '80s, North Melbourne let a young ruckman in their metro zone slip through their fingers. That ruckman happened to be Scott Wynd, Footscray legend who played 237 games, captained the club and won the 1992 Brownlow Medal. When his younger brother Paul came to their attention, North weren't going to make the same mistake, signing him to their list at the age of 15. Paul Wynd's career totalled just three games in 1997. It proved just too hard to break into a Kangaroos forward line featuring Carey, McKernan and Longmire.

Richo: Welcome to the show, Paul.

Paul Wynd: Thanks guys, how are you all?

Billy: You didn't quite reach the heights of your big brother, Paul.

Paul Wynd: I like to say that between the three of us, the old man, my brother and I, we played 242 games and we have one Brownlow Medal.

Covey: We get this little print out every week that has all the details of you career, and it has age on debut which is 21 years and 38 days and then it has age at the time of your last game, 21 years and 58 days. You had a 20-day career.

Paul Wynd: Yeah, well, it was a long time ago, but I'm glad that I did play a few.

Covey: They were in consecutive weeks then obviously.

Paul Wynd: Yes and they were all against interstate clubs. My first game was on a Monday, so I had a long time to wait.

Billy: Paul, where did they play you?

Paul Wynd: I think I started on the forward line but I did do a few stints in the ruck, as well.

Richo: Back in 1997, North Melbourne was a very difficult side to break into. They were the reigning Premiers.

Paul Wynd: They had a very strong club while I was there and it was hard to break into certainly.

Torch: And you would have been running around in that forward line next to Wayne Carey and Pagan's paddock would have been up and going, so did you have to clear out and leave it to Wayne?

Paul Wynd: It was get the ball to Wayne and get everyone out of the way.

Billy: Did you see the year out at North in '97?

Paul Wynd: Yeah, '97 was my last year and I think I lost a bit of passion and a little bit of drive and looking back my commitment and attitude probably wasn't there. I had glandular fever the year before which definitely took a lot out of me and I was probably playing my best footy then.

Torch: How did you get on with Denis Pagan at the time?

Paul Wynd: You had to be on the right side of Denis and I don't think I was one of his favourites. I think big brother had a little bit to do with that.

Covey: So did you used to get advice from Scotty?

Paul Wynd: Little bits and pieces. He was up with the elite group, but he was always there for a short word and so was the old man who played league football as well.

Richo: Paul, tell us about your career as a junior leading up to you being drafted to North.

Paul Wynd: I wasn't actually drafted, I was zoned. Back then zoning was still in place and I was one of the last guys to be zoned as a 15-year-old. I came up through the development sides in the Under 13s and Under 14s and I played school boys with North Melbourne and it just so happened that I was doing work experience down there and Greg Miller pulled me in the office and said, we're thinking about putting you on the list as a 15-year-old so that was a bit of a shock.

Richo: That's a fabulous stamp of approval, Greg Miller, the man who found some of the greatest players of all time thought you were good enough, Paul.

Paul Wynd: Well he missed the mark there a little bit. It was a long time ago and seems like yesterday, so it goes very quickly.

Torch: So how did Scott end up at the Dogs and you ended up at North if you were both in the zone?

Paul Wynd: Well Scott was also zoned to North and I think the rule back then was once you turned 18 you were a free agent and I think one of the secretaries had his birth date wrong. So that's where the baggage comes in but I don't know that he was too keen to go to North Melbourne, I think the Bulldogs looked after him pretty well and as soon as he turned 18, he signed with the Bulldogs.

Covey: It doesn't matter occasionally if North misses out on one because some of the tricks Ron Joseph and Slug Jordon got up to get blokes to North...

Torch: Carey and Longmire to start!

Billy: You said you lost a bit of passion, did you go off playing footy in the bush or anything after that season or did you give it away all together?

Paul Wynd: I had a couple years with Oak Park and a couple of years at Greenvale but I had a knee reconstruction at Oak Park and one on the other leg with Greenvale. And I probably didn't enjoy football as much as I had as a junior.

Billy: Do you follow the footy now?

Paul Wynd: Yeah, I do, I follow the Bulldogs and I follow the Kangaroos and our local side Greenvale and it's just good to see a good game of footy.

Richo: Well Paul, thanks very much for joining us this morning. In your three-game career you played against Adelaide, Fremantle and Sydney.

Billy: What a good way to see some of the country!

Paul Wynd: It would have been nice to play against a Melbourne side.

Covey: But you at least played at Footy Park, the MCG and the SCG.

Paul Wynd: Footy Park was an experience. With 45,000 in the stands and walking down the race and having a few strong words directed towards you it was certainly an experience.

Richo: And one that no one can take away from you Paul thanks so much for joining us this morning.

Paul Wynd: Thanks guys.

Richo: Paul Wynd there, brother of Scott, played for North Melbourne in 1997. How would you be trying to break into the

North Melbourne side as a key marking forward.

Covey: I'm sorry to bring it up Billy because it's been a bitter pill for you for a long time but had you got to play at Geelong and perhaps played three games like Paul, where would you have liked to play your three games?

Billy: Well, Kardinia Park obviously. Then the MCG, and possibly I would have liked to have finished my three games in the then VFL knowing I'd played either Windy Hill or Footscray on a horrible windy wet day so at least I would pride myself in the worst possible conditions you could imagine.

Richo: What about Moorabbin and having a free kick awarded to you in front of the animal enclosure that obviously should have gone the other way!

Torch: And Victoria Park, now that was an experience.

CRAIG BALME

Richmond hardman Neil Balme's nine-year career at Punt Road was already well and truly done when his younger brother Craig followed in his footsteps into the yellow and black jumper. However, after breaking through to the ones in 1983, Craig followed his brother again—this time to Norwood in the SANFL where Neil was coach—ending his VFL career at three appearances. Craig joined us to discuss his footy days and real estate in 2010.

Craig Balme: Good morning guys.

Billy: Where do we find you, Craig?

Craig Balme: I'm living in beautiful Mandurah about 75km south of Perth in Western Australia.

Covey: And your field of endeavour these days, Craig?

Craig Balme: The wonderfully wholesome industry of real estate.

Covey: Oh, well look, given you only played three games of league footy, let's put them to one side. Let's talk real estate. Have you got one open for inspection this morning?

Craig Balme: I've got an auction this morning. A beautiful property.

Billy: Do you have any footy in your life?

Craig Balme: This year we're major sponsors of Peel Thunder in the WAFL.

Champs: Have you got a sign up on the fence, Craig Balme Real Estate?

Craig Balme: Not exactly. We're with a franchise group who I probably can't mention because you're on the ABC!

Richo: Craig, tell us about your footy career. You were 22 years of age when you first played at Richmond. Did they get you across for a season in the magoos first?

Craig Balme: Well, no, I'm surprised you haven't done your research! I moved over with the family when I was eight and Richmond signed me up when I was about 14 or so thinking that I had some talent, probably a mistake of theirs. I played in the Richmond Under 19s when we had that wonderful system of the reserves and seniors and played in the 1980 winning grand final team for the Richmond Under 19s which is obviously the same year Richmond beat Collingwood in the seniors. I actually played against Paul Roos that day, our careers followed very similar tracks didn't they?

Billy: Who was your coach, Craig?

Craig Balme: Wayne Walsh.

Covey: And on that day in 1980 when you played in the Grand Final, you stayed and watched the main game?

Craig Balme: I'm not sure I can remember. We were victorious that day and it was fair to say that I was pretty shabby by half-time of the seconds.

Covey: I would've thought you'd get a pie and a can of brown fizzo.

Craig Balme: No, but I think Don Lane and Bert Newton would remember me because I was with my teammates giving them a bit of lip in the Southern Stand. We were pretty chirpy.

Richo: Craig, tell us about what happened between that grand final day in 1980 when you've won an Under 19s Premiership and your senior debut with Richmond in 1983.

Craig Balme: I had a couple of years in the magoos and then got my chance in the seniors playing at full back. My first game was at Kardinia Park and then one at Arden Street where I played against Kerry Good and actually got in our best that day. We lost but North had two Krakouer brothers running riot. I played pretty darn well and I thought well, this is good, I've got a career set here, I don't have to worry about anything else. And then the following week we played Footscray at the MCG and Simon Beasley kicked 10, I had a very quick reality check that day.

Billy: Given your MCG appearance was in 1983 and given the conditions of today, did you look around when you were on the field and think this is a renovator's dream?

Craig Balme: It's fair to say my head wasn't in real estate at that stage.

Richo: After those three games, how long did you stay at Richmond before you went on to play in SA?

Craig Balme: At the end of that year I left and I went to play for Norwood in Adelaide where I ended up playing for a dozen years and racked up 250 games and played in a Premiership and all that sort of thing.

Champs: Was Neil there at the time?

Craig Balme: Yes, he actually enticed me over. I think it'd be fair to say I wasn't the most mature 22-year-old and didn't handle a few things well at Richmond at the time, some selection decisions and some recruiting decisions that I didn't think were right and, of course, as a 22-year-old I knew everything and decided that wasn't where I wanted to stay.

Billy: Well, it's not the Balme way to just take things on the chin and not make your feelings known Craig.

Craig Balme: Oh, we're not shy, retiring flowers, we tend to manage things in an upfront way, I think it'd be fair to say.

Covey: Occasionally we've seen instances where there'll be a boy playing in a footy team and dad's the coach but when you played at Norwood, your brother was actually coaching you.

Craig Balme: Yeah, he probably coached me for 150 of my 250 games.

Covey: Did he dispense any favours because he was your brother?

Craig Balme: Not that I noticed. He made one glaring error at one stage, he actually dropped me one week. I don't let him forget that.

Richo: Craig, who do you follow in the footy?

Craig Balme: I'm a little on the fickle side. I used to follow Melbourne strongly when my brother was coach but certainly some of their decisions led me to hate them with a passion from a certain day onwards so I'm not a fan of Melbourne anymore, which is probably unfair. And then I actually spent a couple of years in a support role with the Collingwood Football Club when I was living in Melbourne, as a ruck coach under Mick [Malthouse], and that was when Neil was there. And then I was also the inaugural ruck coach at Port Power in their first year in 1997 when I was living in Adelaide, so I've been involved in a little bit of footy. Now we follow Geelong's efforts but I've got a very soft spot for Collingwood because I just love the way they play footy.

Billy: What are you going to do if Geelong and Collingwood end up playing in the Grand Final?

Craig Balme: I can't lose either way!

Torch: So, you haven't been drawn into any of the local WA footy teams, either the Dockers or the Eagles?

Craig Balme: No, having lived in Adelaide for a long time I must admit the idea of a two-team town is not that exciting to me. I love Melbourne where you've got that choice of clubs and teams to watch and follow and just go to a game of footy just for the spectacle rather than having an axe to grind. So, no, I haven't got a leaning either way in that regard. I like it when both Perth teams are struggling and on the bottom because then I get a lot more work done in my office, no one wants to talk football.

Billy: Your number was 36, Craig, and the Tigers haven't given it to a dummy because they've given it to Dustin Martin and he is a very good player.

Craig Balme: Well, again, I haven't kept track of it but have they kept that jumper aside after my three games and waited for Dustin to come along?

Richo: It would have been the lace up, Craig.

Craig Balme: It was a lace up and I also had some very unattractive bright yellow football boots.

Richo: Craig, it's been terrific talking to you this morning. And may you have very busy and productive Monday mornings in your office for years to come as far as we're concerned.

Craig Balme: I'm with you on that, for sure.

Richo: Craig Balme, thanks so much.

Craig Balme: My pleasure.

Finals Fever

PETER JOHNSTON

Peter Johnston was a player with a foot in both camps thanks to notching up 30 games with Melbourne before crossing to Geelong for a further 92 appearances. Apart from thrilling crowds with his high marking, Johnno gained a place in footy folklore as a key player the day Garry Sidebottom missed the bus en route to the 1981 Preliminary Final at VFL Park Waverley.

Peter Johnston: Thanks for having me.

Covey: As was pointed out you came from Melbourne to Geelong, but you're actually from Tasmania, is that right?

Peter Johnston: That's right, I went to St Virgil's. The connection with Melbourne there was the great Stuey Spencer. Now Stuey had coached me for three years in senior footy and there's a story there that I had just come back from Canberra where I'd played rugby union and rugby league for three years and didn't play Aussie Rules. So when I got back to Tassie, it was fourth form or year 10 I think it was Stuey was our senior coach and he reintroduced me to footy. He was great for my development, and just a great bloke and sadly we lost Stuey last year.

Covey: And Johnno, you were renowned for your high leaping, high marking exploits. You wouldn't have done too much of that in rugby union or rugby league?

Peter Johnston: No, all I did was get my ears hurt.

Covey: You weren't in those line outs where they lifted you up were you?

Peter Johnston: Yes, I was. That was interesting but not a game I gravitated to actually.

Richo: GWS and then the Gold Coast have obviously missed the boat there by not getting you into help Karmichael Hunt and Issy Folau!

Covey: Tell us some more about how you got to Melbourne.

Peter Johnston: Yes, I had three years at Melbourne. I had Bobby Skilton for two years, I had Dennis Jones for one and Big Carl. Big Carl decided to move me on actually.

Covey: Now, we thank Johnno over that reference. We had this a couple of weeks ago when someone spoke to us and they only ever said Big Carl. Nothing else was required.

Richo: Tell us about Big Carl, Johnno.

Peter Johnston: Well, I didn't have much to do with Big Carl. He moved me on pretty quickly. That was interesting because the committee came down, it was a week before the season actually was underway, and they've come down to see me and said, 'Look, we're going to move you on and Geelong want to speak to you'. Look, I wasn't happy, but I said I'd speak to Geelong. So I've gone down and met with Geelong and, anyway, I made a handshake agreement and said I'd play with Geelong. So, I'm now committed to Geelong and I get a call on Friday from Ray Biffin who was coaching the seconds and he said, 'Look, we're really short on numbers would you mind playing for us?'

Billy: For the Melbourne seconds?

Peter Johnston: Yes, and I said to him, 'Look Biff, sorry, I've committed to Geelong, I don't think I can'. He said, 'Look, if we ring Geelong and Geelong give you approval, would you play?' And I said, 'Yeah, that'd be fine'. So, Geelong rang me and said yeah, that's okay. So I play and I was Melbourne's best player.

Covey: This is better than the Sidey missing the bus story!

Peter Johnston: Next thing, the committee have rushed down to see me and said, 'Look, would you reconsider?' And I'm saying 'No, no, no, I've made my decision, I'm going'. And all the guys that I played with are all laughing and carrying on. So, I've committed to Geelong and it was two weeks before I got a clearance. And my first game in the seconds down at Kardinia Park was against Melbourne, believe it or not.

Torch: You make a very good case for players having managers these days.

Peter Johnston: Exactly. And the other interesting thing is my first game of football for Melbourne was against North Melbourne in the seconds, right? And I've lined up at centre half-forward, minding my own business and Crackers Keenan is in the ruck. And he's yelled out, 'Johnston!' And I'm thinking I don't know the guy and he doesn't know me, what's he yelling out my name for? And he said, 'Johnston, I'm talking to you'. And I'm looking at him. I'm thinking yeah, right. What do you really want to say? He said, 'I'm gonna rip that jumper off your back. You're a disgrace to that number and that jumper. If you get anywhere near the ball, I'm gonna kick your head off'. And I'm thinking what am I in for here? Turns out Crackers had worn No. 8 at Melbourne so that was the connection.

Covey: You had No. 8 at Melbourne and then you got No. 3 down here. How long did you play in the seconds before you got a senior game?

Peter Johnston: Well, Rod Olsson was coaching in those days so I would have had six or seven games in the seconds and then played the last half in the seniors under Rod. And then Billy Goggin took over in 1980 and I had three years with Bill.

Billy: Did Rod Olsson use you as a forward?

Peter Johnston: Yes, he did. Centre half-forward and full forward mainly.

Billy: Would it be fair to say that the crowd warmed to your exciting high marking but they cooled off a bit when you had a shot for goal?

Peter Johnston: Look, that was bizarre, because I had probably four or five people come down and give me kicking lessons.

Covey: I came down one day from the Addy and had a kick with you!

Peter Johnston: Yeah, you were behind the goals collecting the balls for me! But I had Doug Wade, I had a myriad of people coming through and giving me hints and telling me what to do and, seriously, I had 20-odd thoughts going through my head and I got to the stage where I could not kick 30 metres and it affected me and my game.

Richo: Peter, we have to fast forward through all your 92 games with the Geelong Football Club because the one that most people remember you for is out at Waverley, the Preliminary Final in 1981 when Sidey missed the bus. Tell us your version of the story.

Peter Johnston: Right, my version is that I was one of four players on the interchange. And we're all to meet Saturday morning at the ground and we would be told then whether we're playing or not. But the trouble was that Sidey lived out at Lara. And every time Sidey was picked, we picked him up at Lara. So, the wires got crossed there. Anyway, I've come down to Kardinia Park, and Bill McMaster comes straight to me so I knew straight away that I wasn't playing. Bill came straight over to me and said, 'Look, we've had to go with Sidey', and I said fine. I said, 'Look, I'm not coming up on the bus. I'll drive up'. Kelvin Matthews and Andy Preston were the other two to miss out and they said we'll drive up with Johnno. We got in the car and we're driving up and we were feeling a little bit hungry and, not only that, we were keen punters and we wanted to put a quaddie on. So we stopped off in Glenferrie Road in Hawthorn at the TAB there and next to the TAB there was this chicken and chips shop. I was feeling pretty hungry and decided to hoe into half a chicken and chips and wash it down with a strawberry thickshake. Now that didn't sit too well in the old stomach, especially when I found out I was going to be playing about 60 minutes later, it was brought up pretty quick.

Covey: So, how did you find out you were playing because there were no mobile phones?

Peter Johnston: No, no mobile phones. So, we're driving down Wellington Road, which was horrendous at the best of times, right? The road is chock-a-block and we're just minding our business, having a laugh listening to the races and carrying on. Anyway, we get there probably three quarters of an hour beforehand. And there's Ian McKenzie waving frantically.

Covey: He was the secretary.

Peter Johnston: He's saying you're playing, and I said no I'm not, and he said yes you are because Sidey hasn't turned up. Are you kidding me? I just had half a chicken and chips and a strawberry thickshake, I'm not mentally prepared. And the other thing is Kelvin and Andy both smoked so they were smoking their lungs out in the car. So, I just wasn't mentally prepared for the game. I've got three quarters of an hour to get ready to play in a Preliminary Final.

Richo: All the while, Sidey is still leaning on the gatepost at Lara waiting.

Peter Johnston: And in all seriousness, if he played we would have won. He was a terrific player and I happened to play on him a couple of times when he went to Fitzroy. He was just a great player, but Billy [Goggin] had this thing about him and didn't want to play him for some reason.

Billy: How did you go Johnno, how was your performance?

Peter Johnston: I got zero, zero, zero. I got the Olympic rings!

Covey: Well, that's a classic footy story and you've now heard it from the horse's mouth, Peter Johnston. And, just quickly, you also played here at centre half-forward with Mark Jackson at full forward and there was a game here in the first round of 1984.

Peter Johnston: Yes, that's a famous game because Gary Ablett, Greg Williams and Mick Turner was the centre line. And I played centre half-forward and Jacko played full forward.

Covey: And I reckon Jacko kicked 9.2 and you kicked five straight from centre half-forward.

Peter Johnston: Yes that's right, that's a good memory.

Richo: Peter it's been fantastic talking to you.

Peter Johnston: Thanks guys, it's a pleasure.

Covey: He's just going out for half a chicken and chips and a strawberry thickshake!

HEY, ISN'T THAT IAN McKENZIE?
I THINK HE WANTS SOME OF YOUR CHICKEN!

MARK DWYER

Mark Dwyer was a skinny kid from the Western District when Fitzroy coach David Parkin called his home in Koroit in mid-1986. Parko promised Mark a game in the ones if he came to Melbourne. So Mark came, donned the No. 58 long sleeved Lions jumper and proceeded to take the game by storm. He collected Brownlow votes and finals appearances with ease, and then, it seemed, he was gone, injury preventing him from getting a good run at league footy.

Richo: It was one of the great footy stories. Joining us now on line, one of Koroit's most famous players, Mark Dwyer. Mark, welcome to the Coodabeens.

Mark Dwyer: Good morning gents.

Covey: And I believe Koroit's in the Grand Final.

Mark Dwyer: Yes, today playing Warrnambool and believe it or not, I played for both sides.

Covey: Did you? Did you play under Scotty Turner?

Mark Dwyer: Yeah, I was Scotty's chairman of selectors.

Billy: Where do your allegiances lie today?

Mark Dwyer: A bit mixed actually, maybe 50 cents each way.

Richo: Season '86, you started off playing footy at Koroit and then Parko was coaching the Roys, was he the one who contacted you?

Mark Dwyer: Yes, David contacted me. I did play a couple of practice matches early in the year but then David got in touch with me and actually offered me a senior game to come down and play.

Torch: So that was Round 15, you had the ball 20 times and picked up a Brownlow vote.

Mark Dwyer: That's correct, and I played on Jimmy Buckley.

Covey: How was Jimmy, did he welcome you to league football?

Mark Dwyer: Yeah, he gave me a whack.

Richo: And the way you played and the way you looked captured the imaginations not just of the Fitzroy supporters but I think everyone in footy. You just brought a flair to the way you played, it was a pleasure to watch you play, you were obviously enjoying playing football.

Mark Dwyer: I always enjoyed football. I'm not saying I enjoyed Melbourne, I didn't at all, but playing football was a great love of mine.

Champs: And you were running around I think in No. 58.

Mark Dwyer: That's correct. Yes.

Champs: Did that feel heavy on your back?

Mark Dwyer: Well I don't think they could have found a higher number, but I suppose they didn't think I was going to hang around long.

Covey: So did you travel up and down from Koroit?

Mark Dwyer: Yes I did. I used to travel down on Thursdays and train and play Saturdays.

Covey: And train with Koroit what, Tuesdays?

Mark Dwyer: I trained with Koroit Tuesdays and I actually went back when the VFL had a split round and played with Koroit in between.

Covey: Were you allowed to do that?

Mark Dwyer: Yeah, I was still actually a Koroit player at the time.

Torch: You were playing under what we used to call match permits so how did that system work?

Mark Dwyer: That's correct. I did have to get cleared to Fitzroy after so many games, I can't remember how many it was.

Richo: You played under permit and it was revealed at the end of the season that you'd picked up 10 Brownlow votes for the season including two threes, two best on grounds between Round 15 and the end of the season. Then you found yourself playing finals in your ninth 10th and 11th games for Fitzroy for two wins and one loss.

Mark Dwyer: That's correct, we beat Essendon then Sydney and lost to Hawthorn in the Preliminary Final.

Covey: And what was it like playing in front of that huge crowd at the 'G, it was a long way from down at Koroit with just a few cars around the fence.

Mark Dwyer: It was a fantastic experience. You know, again, to me it was just playing football but the crowds were amazing. And it really is a great buzz, especially around the 'G this time of the year.

Torch: You also played in that momentous game at Waverley

where you won on virtually the last kick of the day when Mickey Conlan kicked that goal.

Mark Dwyer: I played on Hawker I think it was and probably lowered my colours that day and I was rapt to see Mickey pick that ball up and slot it through.

Covey: Then came the Brownlow Medal count and Paul Roos went in as the favourite?

Mark Dwyer: Yes. I don't think Paul's spoken to me since.

Covey: Because you racked up votes very quickly.

Mark Dwyer: Yes, I did. I think I polled in the first four games I played. Look, I was a bit embarrassed, I wasn't the most popular bloke around the Fitzroy Football Club at that time.

Covey: I supposed you can understand the umpires getting you confused with Paul Roos. He was No, 1 and you were No. 58.

Mark Dwyer: Yeah we were about the same height too!

Richo: Mark, all three of those finals games you played were wonderful games of football, full of drama and the game swinging in both directions and played in front of incredibly involved crowds. You must sort of pinch yourself that you had that experience?

Mark Dwyer: It was just absolutely fantastic and now that I've turned 50 I sit back with my wife, who was my girlfriend at the time, and think we can't believe you blokes are still ringing me up!

Billy: And then at the end of that season you chose not to go on the end of season trip with Fitzroy but you went to the races with Koroit.

Mark Dwyer: Yes, I did. I decided to go to the Cox Plate with the Koroit boys.

Billy: Did you see yourself just really as a bush footy player even though you made such an impact in your first season at the Lions?

Mark Dwyer: Yes, I did. I actually spoke to David Parkin last week, I hadn't caught up with him since I finished and I think he knew I was always going to struggle to be a long term prospect down in Melbourne.

Billy: And, unfortunately, your last two seasons in footy weren't as glorious your first. Your second year, they gave you a lower number but you only played a couple games due to a bad injury and then you finished up at St. Kilda, where you had another bad injury, Mark.

Mark Dwyer: I didn't have a lot of luck, I must admit, with an Achilles and a bit of a knee and a few other things. Being 75 kilos ringing wet and playing the way I played with the bigger bodies back in those days didn't suit me much.

Covey: And of course at the same time, there was another Mark Dwyer going around who called himself Mick didn't he?

Mark Dwyer: That's correct, yeah, Mick was at St Kilda at the time and he was at St Kilda for short period while I was there as well.

Covey: Because people always used to say, which Mark Dwyer are you talking about? Oh that Mark Dwyer not Mick Dwyer! So did you end up having a drink with him down at St Kilda?

Mark Dwyer: Yeah, we definitely had a drink together. And I had more hair than him.

Richo: Mark you mentioned you've got divided allegiances between Koroit and Warrnambool, how do you line up with you your VFL/AFL? Before you got the phone call from David Parkin, who'd you barrack for?

Mark Dwyer: I barracked for Carlton.

Champs: And do you still barrack for them to this day? Or is that long gone?

Mark Dwyer: No, my whole family barracks for the Brisbane Lions. And they're one-eyed even if they don't admit it.

Richo: So you're now very much a Lion.

Mark Dwyer: Yeah, we're Lions.

Covey: Yeah, he barracked for Carlton until Jimmy Buckley whacked him!

Mark Dwyer: And don't worry I felt it too, it was a good one!

Covey: Did you get one back?

Mark Dwyer: No, I probably wasn't game but if it was at Koroit he would've got one back! I just told him he had to hit me a lot harder than that. He replied with 'I can'.

Richo: It's been great reminiscing with you Mark, and thanks so much for joining us this morning.

Mark Dwyer: Thanks for remembering me.

Richo: Mark Dwyer there, burst onto the scene with 10 Brownlow votes and three finals for Fitzroy in 1986.

RUDI WEBSTER

One name that still conjures the mysticism and mystery of the VFL in the early 1980s is Rudi Webster. He's probably best remembered as the spark that started the famous fight between Carlton coach Percy Jones and Richmond's Tony Jewell in 1982, but Rudi was a highly successful sports psychologist as well as being a professional cricketer and, later in life, the Ambassador to the USA from his native Barbados. Rudi Webster joined us in 2014.

Richo: A very special guest joins us now from his home in Grenada, Dr. Rudi Webster. Rudi, welcome to the Coodabeens.

Rudi Webster: Thank you very much and greetings from the Caribbean.

Covey: I'm sure there's lots of your friends in Melbourne thrilled to hear your voice on the airwaves.

Rudi Webster: I hope some of them are listening, particularly my friend Percy Jones.

Billy: Have you spoken to Percy in recent times?

Rudi Webster: Not really, but I get the odd message about him from some of my friends over there.

Covey: Having mentioned Percy Jones perhaps you'd better

start with talking footy here and we often say when you have a bit of word association and you mentioned the name Rudi Webster, people mainly say Percy Jones and Tony Jewell, the blue out at Waverley. What's your recollection of that famous footy incident?

Rudi Webster: Well, in 1979, I was at the Carlton Football Club and at the end of the season, Richmond finished near the bottom and they asked me if I would come and help them in the 1980 season. And you know how much Richmond and Carlton loved each other in those days, so when I went over to Richmond, I wasn't a very popular guy at the Carlton club and we did fairly well, we actually got to the finals. I think it was the Preliminary Final, Carlton was playing against Richmond and in the first quarter, we knocked them around pretty badly. I think two or three of them had a slight concussion by the end of the first quarter. And when we were in the quarter-time break, I was with the Richmond huddle and Percy was going towards the Carlton huddle and he looked in my direction and saw me smiling and talking to some of the guys and he was pretty angry. So, he changed direction and started to come towards our huddle and he started to mouth off, you know, you turncoat, etc, and as he got a bit closer, his language became more colourful. Tony Jewell was very surprised about this and when I looked up I saw Tony's eyes—when Tony got angry, his eyes used to roll around in circles, right? And I saw his eyes rolling and I thought oh no, not in front of 80,000 people and millions of viewers on TV in Australia, they're not really going to fight are they?

Champs: And you would have had a front row seat!

Rudi Webster: Well, before those thoughts could get out of my mind, they were throwing punches at each other. Eventually, they were parted and Jones was still very upset, I think his team was pretty upset too. But we got our guys back to the basics and to attack the ball and to continue playing the tough, rough football that we started. So, it wasn't a match after that because their minds were not on the game. At the end of the game, some of the reporters came up and they tried to make a racial issue out of this thing and I said no, Percy Jones is my best friend in Australia, along with Wes Lofts. And the next day we went on to Channel 7, on *World of Sport* with Lou Richards, Tony Jewell asked me to come to the station with him. Lou had the two coaches on and he asked them what really happened up there and they, of course, wouldn't give satisfactory answers. So Lou invited me onto the set and he said, Rudi, could you tell us what happened, I said, 'I really don't know, but this is the first time I've had two white men fighting over me'.

Richo: Everyone remembers that incident and you've retold it so beautifully for us. But it's such a small part of your remarkable career in in sports medicine. You originally trained as a medical doctor, is that right?

Rudi Webster: That's right, yes.

Richo: What got you interested in the sports psychology side of things?

Rudi Webster: Well, I used to play professional cricket in England for Warwickshire and I was in a live human laboratory, I was seeing everything that was going on, you know, all the problems that players are having. And I used to talk to them and they said to me, 'Rudi, you are good at this thing, why don't you take it up professionally?' and I said, 'Ah, no, no, no'. But then when I came to Melbourne, I got the opportunity to work with some of the football clubs, Carlton first and Richmond and then Melbourne, and then Essendon and I helped Allan Jeans at Hawthorn prepare his team mentally for the 1983 Grand Final. I got involved in that and I was doing pioneering work with the mental preparation of the players because in those days, nobody was thinking about that it was all about muscle and brawn and being tough and stuff like that. So I did that very successfully and then I worked with the West Indies cricket team under Clive Lloyd and we had

MAKE A WISH BOYS!
HARV

tremendous success there. I think, the mental component of performance had been neglected up until then, well it was used in a different sort of way, it wasn't used in a very scientific and constructive way.

Torch: When did you leave Melbourne, Rudi?

Rudi Webster: I left Australia in 1986, I went back to work with my Prime Minister in Barbados to use some of those techniques to help him to improve the performance of the public service. And then eventually, I went to Washington as the Barbados' Ambassador to the United States. And that led to other things. So that is a capsule of what I did after I left Australia.

Covey: Rudi, was it you who made the Bombers players lie on the floor and hold hands and Ronnie Andrews and Crackers Keenan weren't all that keen on the idea?

Rudi Webster: No, that was somebody else. But Kevin Sheedy was the best coach I worked with and he gave me a free hand to do all sorts of things. The Grand Final in 1984, Hawthorn had beaten Essendon the year before, and they'd beaten them in the normal games during the season. Before that Grand Final, for about two weeks, I got the players to mentally rehearse, and I don't know why I did this, being four goals down at three-quarter time, and then getting them to visualise themselves playing really aggressive and efficient football in the last quarter. And lo and behold, you wouldn't believe this, at the end of the third quarter after Hawthorn had knocked us around physically, we were four goals down. And at three-quarter time, Kevin was a bit angry at some of the fellows and one of them said 'Look, coach, we rehearsed this situation with Rudi several times, we know what we have to'. So at the first bounce of the ball, Watson or somebody gathered the ball and the drive started from there. And I think we outplayed them in the last quarter and won the match.

Champs: They kicked 9.6 for the quarter!

Rudi Webster: That's right. It was really an incredible performance.

Richo: Rudi, in reviewing your latest book, *Think Like A Champion*, the great Wes Hall, quotes you saying that you'd never come across a great player who wasn't also a great thinker.

Rudi Webster: That's right and when I say a great thinker, I don't mean an academic thinker. There is a huge difference between academic intelligence or academic thinking and sports intelligence or sports thinking. I mean, look and see how many scholars and academics become good sportsmen, it's totally different. But all of the great champions are tremendous thinkers, they think very simply, they can identify the important priorities they have to face and then they make the right decisions, and they execute the basics really very well. And that is what I've tried to do with all the sporting teams and the sportsmen that I've had.

Covey: What about with a team like Fremantle, last year, for example, they made the Grand Final against Hawthorn and they missed some shots for goal early and it's often said that the occasion got to them, it's their first time there, the nerves have got them. How do you go about mentally preparing a team for a big occasion that they're unaccustomed to?

Rudi Webster: Well, one of the good things about mental preparation and visualisation is that you can sit in your bed or on your toilet seat or in your car or wherever and visualise the things you want to happen. You can visualise yourself dealing with the setbacks that you're going to have on the field and you discuss these things before they get out on the field and you mentally rehearse them so that when they actually happen on the field, they're not caught unexpectedly and then they know exactly how to cope with them. One of the things that Peter Thomson, the great golfer, used to say to me about confidence is that it is about knowing what you are doing and being in control of what you're doing. If you're not in control of what you're doing, your confidence can go. And I suspect that when Fremantle missed those goals and things didn't go the way they expected, they realised that they were not in control of what they were doing and then of course, their confidence fell. And once it starts to fall, if you don't arrest it, it can fall and affect just about every aspect of your game. I don't know if that is what happened to Fremantle but this is where the mental preparation helps you to anticipate these things, and deal with them before the game actually starts; to deal with them mentally before the game starts.

Covey: I'm actually just looking at the program that's coming on after us, Rudi, features former Carlton captain Mark Maclure.

Rudi Webster: Yes.

Billy: Can you recall working with Mark at Carlton? Anything, known?

Rudi Webster: Well, not on the field but off the field, possibly!

Richo: Rudi, you've made a tremendous effort to share the knowledge you've accumulated over decades across a range of sports and a range of countries in your new book, *Think Like A Champion.*

Rudi Webster: I was asked to write the book by, believe it or not, some Indian cricketers, and so I wrote it and it was published in Delhi in India. And I'm really very proud of it because I've drawn information from the 30 or 40 years that I was involved in sport. A lot of it, funnily enough, is about Aussie football, about Sheedy and Barassi and Tony Jewell and people like that and even young Malthouse. When Malthouse first started with Footscray, he was with the Richmond team, so I knew him very well, but I could see the enormous potential that he had as a leader and a coach and as he went on he didn't disappoint me. I thought he could have won a few more Premierships.

Champs: He hasn't given up.

Rudi Webster: No, he hasn't given up and he's working with Carlton now!

Torch: You've come full circle.

Covey: He might get you back!

Rudi Webster: I think he needs more help.

Richo: Rudi, it's been wonderful talking with you. Thank you so much. And your influence on Australian football goes way beyond a fight between Tony Jewell and Percy Jones at Waverley.

Rudi Webster: Well, thank you very much and it was a pleasure talking to you.

Richo: All the very best thanks again, Dr. Rudi Webster from his home in Grenada, even though he's originally from Barbados.

The Seconds' Brownlow

BILL SHELTON

The Gardiner Medal was first awarded to the best and fairest player in the VFL in 1926 and continued all the way until 1999. As Digger would say, that's a very long time. Bill Shelton played 12 senior games in his career at Hawthorn between 1957 and 1959 but he is best remembered for winning the Gardiner Medal in 1959.

Richo: First question, Bill. Where's your Gardiner Medal? Where do you keep it?

Bill Shelton: I haven't got it. I gave it to the footy club. I gave it to the historical museum at the football club.

Covey: Did you, though, for some years flash it around a bit when you had dinner parties at home, Bill?

Bill Shelton: Well, in actual fact, Ian, there's quite a story about that because I never got it. And another interesting little point to this whole thing was that I was a wool buyer in those days and I must tell you about training at Geelong.

Covey: Did we miss out on you?

Bill Shelton: You did! Thank goodness, I would have been a bit more lead in the saddle. Anyway, I was driving up to Albury, it must have been in the finals because it was '59 and

Hawthorn seconds won the flag as you know, too. And I'm sitting in the back, a 22- or 23-year-old fellow… reading the sporting page. We were little interested in anything else and here's a note in the paper that says young Hawk wins Gardiner Medal and I said, good heavens, I've won the Gardiner Medal and I didn't think anything about it. I get back to training on Thursday night very late and some official said to me, 'Oh Bill you've won the Gardiner Medal'. I said, 'I know, I read about it. You're a bit late with the news, old boy!'

Richo: And where did the medal actually go after it was awarded to you?

Bill Shelton: I just didn't ever get it and, as a matter of interest, I have a nice little story. I was a director for the RACV for many, many years and all these directors used to tease me about where's the medal. Unbeknownst to me, one of them wrote to the league and said, 'Look, you know, Shelton never got his medal'. And I didn't know that fact at the time. Anyway, eventually I got a call from [Hawthorn president] Ian Dicker about 10 years ago and he said, 'Bill we want you to be a special guest at a Hawthorn-West Coast game'. I thought, this is pretty nice. He said, 'Bring your wife' and I said, 'Oh, that's even better'. So, I get out to the football ground and we're ushered into the VIP lunch before the game with all these West Coast committee and Hawthorn committee and Ian said, 'Look you're sitting on the head table, Bill'. I said, 'Oh don't be silly'. Anyway, I was and there was the president of West Coast and exalted Hawthorn people like Knightsy and Lethal. I couldn't believe it. Lunch went on and, to cut a long story short, Ian got up and said, 'Look the League have apologised and are going to correct an omission that occurred some years ago', and I still didn't know what was going on, 'and we're going to give Bill Shelton his Gardiner Medal'.

Billy: You know what probably happened? You've won the Gardiner Medal and they said, where's Bill? Oh, look, he's classing out there in Hamilton. So, they sent it to Hamilton but you'd left there to go to Meredith and it's been chasing you around regional Victoria ever since!

Bill Shelton: You're absolutely right. I didn't train at Hawthorn much in those times because I was at wool sales in Albury and Adelaide and Geelong. I trained a lot down at your team, Ian, with a very nice fellow, Tom Morrow.

Covey: Yeah, Tommy was a terrific fellow.

Bill Shelton: I always enjoyed playing against Geelong because I'd get a lot of kicks because I knew all their names! Oh, leave it, Harry, leave it, I've got it covered Harry! And Harry would leave it and make a complete idiot of himself!

Richo: Bill, you finished up at Hawthorn in '59. Just two years later, Hawthorn finished on top of the letter and won the flag. Could you see the seeds of that side in the young players you would have been playing with through '57 to '59?

Bill Shelton: You could almost because we won the flag in the twos in '58 and again in '59 so we had a pretty good team. And I wasn't very good. It was a bit like coming up against Federer in the tennis because I had to put up with Brendan Edwards in the middle. He was worth about three blokes.

Richo: And Brendan was one of the first modern footballers, taking fitness to a new level.

Bill Shelton: He really was a sensational player and his fitness was at a completely new level. He really was fabulous. If Brendan and the opponent were running for the ball, nine out of 10 times Brendan would get it.

Torch: The other thing that you had to do there was live in the shadow of John Kennedy who was coaching the seniors then but who was coaching the reserves at the time?

Bill Shelton: Tubby Edmonds, a terrific fellow. And…

Covey: Not talked about enough, Tubby Edmonds.

Bill Shelton: Anyway, he was a terrific bloke, he moulded us into not a bad team in '58 and '59.

Billy: When you first arrived, they gave you No. 40. It only took them a season to realise they'd better get you up the list a bit and gave you No. 7 for your last two seasons.

Covey: Wow, a single digit.

Bill Shelton: Yeah. Well, there was another mistake Hawthorn made.

Billy: Who took seven after you Bill?

Bill Shelton: Ian Law.

Covey: Liberty Law.

Bill Shelton: Yeah, good company. I told Liberty not to let it down. And he didn't.

Billy: Do you still get down to the club, Bill?

Bill Shelton: I mean, we always have a reunion once or twice a year. And I think this year, there'll be a lot of reunions because it's 50 years, of course, since the '61 flag. These blokes that played in '61 reckon they set up the first flag but that's not true. Those little blokes in '58 and '59 did. It was the first flag ever to come to Hawthorn in the history of the club.

Richo: Up until that time, Hawthorn had been a power in the VFA and then, after being admitted into the VFL in the 1920s, they spent about 30 years really being a chopping block.

Bill Shelton: Oh, totally. I think, in actual fact, in the early '50s there were a couple of seasons where they hardly won a game. And the view was the league would toss Hawthorn out and give that slot to Coburg which was the growth corridor of

Melbourne. It's been a wonderfully successful club since that late '50s period.

Covey: It's interesting, Bill, that a lot of people have won Gardiner Medals. And people have a bit of a guffaw about it and say the winners are never heard of again, but it didn't hold you back from carving out a successful career in real estate.

Bill Shelton: Well, that's right. But Ian, I have to tell you, when I was a wool buyer in '59 or '60, I was with William Horton and Co, and the chairman asked me to come and see him. And I thought, gee, what have I done now? I don't think I've pinched any money or anything. Anyway, the chairman said, 'Bill, I think you had better make up your mind whether you want to be a league footballer or be a wool buyer'. So, I went home and said to my mother, 'I've had the wood put on me as to whether I should be a wool buyer or a league footballer', and she said, 'Darling, I think you'd better be a wool buyer!'

Richo: But, of course, if that question was put to a young man today, the opposite selection would be made in a heartbeat.

Bill Shelton: Companies encourage young blokes today to play whereas in those days I could never get to training because we were always working late. While I'm here, can I tell you about a great trick you might be interested in? All young blokes should take notice of this. I wasn't very fit so I used to put my ankles in about six inches of warm water in the bath before I went out to play and then put my bandages and socks on. There'd be all these idiots, you know, doing four or five laps to warm up and I'd just go to the centre and chat with the umpire and tell him what a great bloke he was!

Torch: That's how you win a Gardiner!

Covey: In that year you won the Gardiner, did you play many senior games?

Bill Shelton: I think I only played one.

Covey: And can you remember how many votes you polled?

Bill Shelton: I think it might have been 21 or something like that.

Billy: After you finished at Hawthorn, you didn't continue playing football anywhere at all. You just concentrated on your career.

Bill Shelton: I did actually. I had a few offers asking me to go and coach but I didn't. Footy was great and we had a super time but I didn't think I was quite a committed player.

Covey: Wasn't there an old boys' team you could've played for Bill?

Bill Shelton: Well, I was a boarder at Ivanhoe Grammar all my life. I think they were in D Grade so I might have got a kick there.

Richo: And how do you like the young Hawks today?

Bill Shelton: Oh, fabulous, fabulous. We couldn't hold a candle to what these fellows do today. We trained twice a week and, as I say, I was generally in the country running a few laps with a crook old pair of sandshoes. We didn't take it very seriously but we had a lot of fun. Yeah. And Ian and Billy, I was very grateful to your team to let me train at Geelong.

Billy: Ah, well, we've always been a very caring, sharing club.

Bill Shelton: And they used to look after us in those days, you know, you always went into the opposition room and the umpire, too, and we made a hell of a mess of ourselves.

Covey: Hey, good to see you, Bill.

Bill Shelton: Thank you. A great honour to be invited.

Covey: I see Bill around town from time to time and often make reference to you being a Gardiner Medallist so it's good to be able to actually hear the story behind it.

Bill Shelton: Thanks awfully.

Richo: Thank you for joining us this morning on the Coodabeen Champions. Bill Shelton, won the Gardiner Medal playing for Hawthorn in 1959.

Bill Shelton: I suppose you can say umpires have always made mistakes!

BILL VALLI

The late 70s and early '80s was a golden period for West Australians trying their luck in the VFL. And it wasn't just kids coming across the Nullabor, established players with long track records in the WAFL were heading east, too. One such player was Bill Valli who spent two seasons in Victoria at Collingwood and then Essendon, having moved at the ripe old age of 29. He won a Gardiner Medal for the Bombers in his second year, 1980.

Richo: Welcome to the Coodabeens Bill.

Bill Valli: Thanks very much.

Billy: Congratulations on your Gardiner, sorry we haven't caught up with you sooner, Bill!

Bill Valli: That's quite ok, it's long time ago, I think I finished at Essendon in 1980.

Richo: Well, we remember you well because people used to call you Frankie, of course.

Bill Valli: Amongst other things. There was Rudi as well.

Champs: What about Moonee?

Bill Valli: Yes, that too, anything you like.

Torch: You must have been a fair age when you came over here because you had a long career in the West.

Bill Valli: Yes, I came over when I was 29. The first time I came over was actually when Tuddenham and Thompson were big stars. Peter Eakins went to Collingwood in about '71 and I was a brash 21-year-old not playing much here and I went to Collingwood as well and then came back. Then a decade later I'd had an ambition to go and play in Melbourne for many, many years and the chance came. At 29 it's a bit dangerous and I was getting on but they gave me a chance, and they were a great club. After a year and a bit I was passed on to Essendon and fortunately, they gave me a chance too. My form wasn't brilliant, but it was a great experience in Melbourne.

Covey: Everyone goes on about James Podsiadly playing footy at 29. You were the James Podsiadly of the '70s, Bill.

Bill Valli: Farmer played until he was 35–36, Cable played into his thirties as did Mal Whinnen and Bill Dempsey. So it was possible but you've just got to have the right body and the interest but you know, I think I finished up at 32 at Subiaco here.

Billy: Do you recall who polled behind you in that 1980 Gardiner?

Bill Valli: I honestly don't. I played about eight games with Essendon. I roved to Justin Madden coming through and Roger Merrett. I was roving to them. So that's probably why I got a few votes. I wasn't playing well enough to get in the seniors. Bernie Sheehy was the seconds coach at the time and Barry Davis was just bailing out of Essendon with Kevin Sheedy coming in towards the end of the year, but both clubs were magnificent to me and I have a lot of good memories.

Covey: So you won your Gardiner Medal under Bernie Sheehy, well Bernie's still coaching by the way, coaching Ajax in the Amateurs.

Bill Valli: Well if you see him, I've got a little pewter mug he gave me, he was a very nice bloke to me. I was 30-and-a-bit then, but he was respectful of my contribution. And I probably got a few handballs and used to get under the ruckman and get the hardball. I didn't go to Melbourne to be the best seconds player, but as it was, I was really quite grateful.

Champs: Something we ask all our Gardiner Medallists is how did you find out you'd won Bill?

Bill Valli: Gee, I honestly don't know. I know I jogged around the MCG with Kelvin Templeton, that was the year he won the Brownlow. But I was just told that I had won I guess.

Richo: And there would have been a third because back then the Brownlow, the Gardiner and the Morrish all jogged around. Do you remember who was the Morrish Medallist?

Bill Valli: No.

Torch: It was somebody called P. Lane from Richmond.

Covey: That would be Peter Lane, I think he was a forward.

Billy: And have you still got your Gardiner kicking around there Bill?

Bill Valli: I have, yes, and I've got Bernie's cup here, which I'm looking at right now. I was just in awe of their kindness and Bernie particularly acknowledging my contribution albeit small to Essendon at the time.

Torch: Bill, your early career at West Perth would have meant that Polly would have been your coach?

Bill Valli: Yes, he was my first coach and I was 18 or 19 and played on a wing with him and he'd handball the ball out to me. Just a great bloke and he was 32 at the time then but West Perth and Western Australia generally had had a lot of good players over the previous two or three decades prior to joining the VFL.

Billy: You played 17 games for Collingwood and in 1979 picked up four Brownlow votes.

Bill Valli: Hafey had me on the bench four or five times and I had higher expectations. I had a muscle hernia injury, I trained very hard in '79 running around the streets of Wembley Downs over here where I lived and strained my stomach muscles and couldn't get over that. But when you play football and you jump onto the oval, you're equal and I was just disappointed with not being able to go flat out but I still enjoyed it. And I had great admiration for Collingwood as a club as well.

Billy: Do you follow either of Collingwood or Essendon, Bill?

Bill Valli: Just generally from a distance. Once I got out of football, I regretfully didn't have much involvement other than as a normal bystander and what I would see and read and love the game. And I wish that the Eagles and Dockers could do a lot better. I think we've regressed in the last five or 10 years but we have a lot of potential skill in Western Australia. It's just a matter of putting it all together.

Richo: Well, we've got to ask you this question Bill and you can answer safely and confidently because if anyone's listening in Perth, there's not very many of them. You're sitting there in Perth, you've got to make a choice: Eagles or Dockers?

Bill Valli: Honest to god neither. I just follow the footy generally, I've got no passion, other than just the love of the game from a bygone era and I want to see them both do well. I just believe greatly in Western Australia and I'm sad that we've come back a notch or two because I felt that we could dominate and we did in that first five to 10 years but have fallen back.

Covey: I was just looking at your stats from that year at Collingwood, which were very impressive and they gave you the No. 2 jumper so they obviously thought highly of you. You kicked 17 goals and 29 behinds Bill!

Bill Valli: Well I was never a great set shot, I was a better kick on the run. But I came across to Melbourne with rubber stops and I think the first day at Victoria Park we played Fitzroy and they crushed us and I ended up with shingles the next week. And I played with bloody shingles for a few weeks but I learned that you can't play in Melbourne successfully with rubber stops. You learn quickly though at 29 that you don't have many excuses to make anymore.

Covey: It's been lovely to talk to you, Bill.

Bill Valli: Thanks for the opportunity, guys. It's great to be part of the show and here's hoping the West Australian contingent can kick a bit of arse over there as the year continues.

Richo: Them's fighting words! Well, you have a good time at the Dockers game on Monday and thanks for talking with us.

Bill Valli: My pleasure, guys. Thanks very much.

Richo: Bill Valli who won the Gardiner Medal in 1980 wearing an Essendon jumper.

DARYL VERNON

Daryl Vernon played just nine games with Richmond—either side of eight games with Sydney—but he still managed to etch his name in VFL history by winning the Gardiner Medal in 1981.

Daryl Vernon: Thanks for the welcome. I grew up listening to you guys and it amazes me that you're still going so strong.

Richo: It's terrific to hear you going so strong as well, Daryl. The year that you won your Gardiner was the year we first started doing this show, 1981.

Daryl Vernon: I thought about it the other day, 30 years ago, I can remember when I was 21 I used to look at these older players hanging around footy clubs and I've turned into one now.

Richo: What's on your agenda for today, Daryl?

Daryl Vernon: I follow my boys at the moment. They're both quite competent footballers and they've just changed clubs to Leongatha. And I'm heading over to Traralgon for their first game today. I wish I could show you that I'm standing in front of 10 cows who've come over thinking they're gonna get fed out of the car.

Billy: Your Gardiner year, was that your first year at the Tiges?

Daryl Vernon: No, I grew up in the Mt Waverley area in the times when we had zoning with the club. So, I grew up barracking for Richmond and fortunately went through the thirds and the reserves etc. I think I started about '77 or '78 playing thirds, and I'm pretty disappointed that they still don't have those sort of competitions any more. The first year I think I Donny Davenport was coach and the next, it was Paddy Guinane.

Richo: Daryl, you're altogether too modest. Of course, in your career at the Under 19s at Richmond, you also won a Morrish Medal.

Daryl Vernon: Well , that's to be disputed, too! It was funny but I was rung up one night by one of my best friends who was playing for Fitzroy at the time and we both drew with another chap from the Kangaroos. Anyway, what happened was, I said seeing you were there at the count, did anyone mention I got reported? And apparently it didn't come up. So I was keeping it hush hush and I hung on to it for about three days and then they found out and took it off me again! And that was one of those reports where you really didn't do much but they thought they'd give you a week anyway.

Richo: And who were your two co-medallists that year?

Daryl Vernon: That was in the thirds, and one was Andrew McPhee from Fitzroy and the other guy was Steve Simpson who passed away tragically about three weeks ago. And he was playing for North Melbourne then.

Richo: So that time when you were down at Richmond it must have been pretty exciting because they'd been bumping along not going very well and then came from nowhere to win the 1980 flag.

Daryl Vernon: When you still had Graeme Richmond involved at Richmond it certainly had the ship sailing pretty straight. We had a lot of good players. I mean, Kevin Bartlett's still playing, we went and recruited Rob Wiley from Western Australia after winning seven best and fairests over there. So, we had a lot of good little blokes and you have your David Clokes and I think that was the year Roachy took that mark of the year. But I grew up barracking for Richmond and I set myself a goal of playing one game for them and I played a few more, but it was a great club to be involved with at that time.

Billy: Well, yours was a boy's own dream, Daryl, but what happened in '82? You've won the Gardiner and you've played a few games in the ones in '81 but what happened in '82 for you?

Daryl Vernon: Well, the way I remember it was Richmond had won the flag in 1980 and it was always going to be a hard team to break into and I broke in in '81. You had Barry Rowlings, Robbie Wiley, Kevin Bartlett, Paul Sarah jumped in there, Dale Weightman. I had about five guys I had to get in front of. So, I played a few games and then I snapped the hamstring pretty severely and all I wanted to do at that stage in my life is play ones and I did a trip around Australia at the end of the '81 season with my girlfriend and we ended up over in Perth and, next minute, I was swapped with South Fremantle and Richmond got Maurice Rioli. I'll leave you to work out who won in that one!

Billy: Poor old Tiges, dudded again!

Torch: And then out of the blue in '83 you ended up playing for the Swans.

Daryl Vernon: I kept my bags packed and we ended up living up there and that was a great experience for a couple of years.

Torch: You were there right at the start of the Swans' adventure in Sydney.

Daryl Vernon: I think I was their first ever recruit to be taken by Sydney outside of the listed players they went up with. That might be something I could hang my hat on later in life.

Richo: Talking trivia questions Daryl, you came back and had another season in Richmond after playing up there in Sydney and in that final season you managed to snag a best on the ground. Three Brownlow votes for one of the games.

Daryl Vernon: And I think I came home and I thought to myself, well you can die happy now, I was pretty happy to get three Brownlow votes. I came off the bench, they put me in the back pocket which wasn't my regular position. I finished off that season at the Tigers and thoroughly enjoyed all my football career to be honest.

Richo: Well Daryl, we're mindful we need to let you hop back in the car and continue your drive over the mountains to Traralgon but, just before you go, you mentioned one of the great legends in the history of Australian football, the late Graeme Richmond. What are your memories of him?

Daryl Vernon: When I was a younger person we used to hear a lot of stories—whether they were true or not—that Graeme was a straight shooter. He was a 10-round boxer so you looked him in the eyes and you're petrified to look away in case he would pull you back straight in line. He would come up to me on occasions and say remember that game out at Waverley two years ago, you absolutely burnt it out there. He pulled back games where I didn't even realise he was watching me, you know, and he had an aura about him. I remember reading one day that if we had our own Churchill over here, maybe Graeme Richmond would have been that one with the way he could lead men.

Richo: Fantastic, wonderful days, Daryl. Safe driving down the hill to Traralgon and have a great day watching your boys play for the Parrots this arvo.

Daryl Vernon: Well, may your careers continue on as well. Thanks for making me feel a little bit older than I did before.

The year after we interviewed Daryl, one of the sons he spoke of going to watch play for the Leongatha Parrots, Beau, suffered a major on-field injury leaving him quadriplegic. Beau has since gone on to be one of country football's most accomplished coaches with Leongatha and his hometown, Phillip Island.

MALCOLM REED

Our interview with Daryl Vernon about winning the 1981 Gardiner Medal turned up the fact that we had overlooked co-winner of the Gardiner that year. Setting us straight was, in fact, the other winner Malcolm Reed from Geelong, who contacted our producer Young Andy. He quickly lined up Malcolm to join us on the show.

Richo: Good morning, Malcolm. Tell us about what happened, were you sitting at home listening to the show and all of a sudden your year came up?

Malcolm Reed: Yeah, that's right. I just heard Daryl talking there and I thought there might have been a mention of a co-winner that year being that it was the same year the countback system was taken away for the Brownlow.

Covey: So, what happened with the Gardiner that year, Malcolm?

Malcolm Reed: I understand that Daryl Vernon would have won it on the old countback system. When we drew, I think Les Bailey, the reserves team manager, made representations to the club that because the Brownlow countback arrangement had been taken away and it was whoever had the same number of votes were going to win the medal. So, Les made representations to the Geelong committee and I believe they went to the VFL and it was changed.

Billy: And so much so Malcolm, you actually ran around the ground as joint winner of the Gardiner Medal with Daryl. It's funny that Daryl didn't remember that.

Champs: Yeah Daryl! What were you thinking?

Malcolm Reed: There was a whole gang of us running around given it was Bernie Quinlan and Barry Round [Brownlow Medallists] and Daryl and me, two sets of joint winners.

Covey: That's 1981, and Geelong won the reserves that year as well didn't they?

Malcolm Reed: Yes, we won the game just before we did the lap of the oval. I'd had a glass of champagne or two before I ran around the ground.

Covey: So, the rest of the boys were in the rooms celebrating the flag and you're out running around before the main game.

Malcolm Reed: That's right. I had to go over to the cricket change rooms in the bottom of the Ponsford stand to get some clean gear and then go run around the ground and miss out on some of those celebrations.

Billy: From memory Malcolm, you wore No. 1?

Malcolm Reed: That's correct.

Covey: Who did you take that over from?

Malcolm Reed: I couldn't be sure but I think it was Wayne Closter but it was a bit of a surprise to be given that low number in early '78.

Billy: Well, you kicked on after that Gardiner Medal year because '82 through to your career ending down at the Cats in

’85, you racked up a fair few games, ’83 in particular I think you played almost the whole season including some Brownlow votes.

Malcolm Reed: Yeah, I don’t remember exactly where I scored the votes, but I think I scored some against St Kilda down at Kardinia Park one day and against Collingwood at Victoria Park.

Billy: Well, if you don’t remember that’s okay. Because Daryl Vernon probably does!

Covey: And did you kick the winning goal for Geelong against Fitzroy one day?

Malcolm Reed: Last game of 1979. I think Fitzroy had to win it to stay in the finals. We were five goals down at about the 20-minute mark of the last quarter. We kicked three quick goals. Kelvin Matthews kicked a goal from centre half-forward. I’ve never heard so much noise in my whole life. And then I was fortunate enough to get hold of the footy with a minute or two to go and put it through.

Covey: I reckon you might have been out in front of the social club.

Malcolm Reed: I was in the pocket in front of the social club.

Covey: And you slotted it calmly for a goal but the crowd went berserk. It was fantastic stuff.

Billy: Malcolm, my colleague Ian here was a trainer down at Geelong about that time. Did you bump into Cove?

Malcolm Reed: The memory I do have of him is when I was playing Under 19s down there, it was the end of the 1975 season, we had an Under 19 footy trip to Hobart. And Ian came on that trip. And he interviewed all the hostesses on the flight with the swizzle sticks for the drinks, it was very amusing.

Covey: We discovered the delights of apple cider in Tasmania, I think, Malcolm. You and Paul Jeffreys.

Malcolm Reed: Shane Dillon was there.

Covey: Yeah, the late Shane Dillon. Gee, he was a tough footballer.

Malcolm Reed: Yeah, he was amazing.

Billy: And where did you go after you left the Cats at the end of '85?

Malcolm Reed: Actually, I was still there in '86 and '87. But I had a groin injury and then I hurt a shoulder and I sort of missed the '86 season. I played until Round 7 in the seconds in '87. And then I got a bit petulant and quit because I wasn't sure that I was going to be considered for a game. I went to Bacchus Marsh for a couple of years, had a year off and then went back and played with Inverleigh, the old Leigh Districts, for two years which is where I came from originally.

Billy: Still involved in footy, Malcolm?

Malcolm Reed: No, I haven't been involved since I played in those days.

Covey: Follow the Cats?

Malcolm Reed: Yes, the game last night was pretty interesting. Halfway up light tower 4 I think we were sitting.

Covey: That's no way to treat a Gardiner Medallist!

Billy: No! Where is your Gardiner, Malcolm?

Malcolm Reed: It will be in a box in a cupboard here somewhere.

Richo: How would you go if you just turned up at one of the turnstiles of the MCG and produced the Gardiner Medal, how far would it get you?

Billy: You know what the green coat would say? He'd say 'You're not Daryl Vernon!'

Torch: After you've done that lap around the ground, there's no chance you got off and had a couple of drinks with Roundy is there?

Malcolm Reed: No, I don't think that happened. The last memory I have of Barry Round, I ran the Rip to River one year, '89, Point Lonsdale to Ocean Grove, and Barry Round just ran past me and beat me by a kilometre.

Covey: He used to go down on holidays and run that every year. It's in January and I reckon Roundy went past me one year, too. He was a marvel. It's been fantastic to catch up with you, Malcolm.

Malcolm Reed: Thank you, Ian.

Billy: And thanks for setting the record straight.

Richo: It was very good of you to get in touch with us because now we've got it straight. The 1981 Gardiner Medal, there were two struck because it was a tie between yourself and Daryl Vernon.

Malcolm Reed: That's it.

Billy: And get the medal out of mothballs, wear it around your neck next time you go to the footy!

Malcolm Reed: I'll turn up to your OB van one day wearing it.

INDEX

D

E

F

G

H

I

J

K

L

V

W

Y

Z